How to Sell Your Home in 5 Days

SECOND EDITION

BILL EFFROS

WORKMAN PUBLISHING · NEW YORK

Casa Bella
New Hope, Pennsylvania

Sold!

T he owners of this house sent me this picture after selling their home in
five days. The home was owned by a developer who taught real estate at
the Wharton School of Business and his wife, a real estate broker.
Professionally they've sold over 3,000 homes.

They were unable to sell their own home until they tried the 5-Day
Method.

Here's part of the note that accompanied the picture:

"The 5-Day Method really works! I feel like an anvil has been taken off my chest."

{Every ad in this book resulted in a 5-Day sale.}

Library of Congress
Cataloging-in-Publication Data
Effros, Bill G.
How to sell your home in 5 days
Second Edition
by Bill G. Effros.
p.   cm.
ISBN-13: 978-0-7611-0960-0
ISBN-10: 0-7611-0960-9
1. House Selling. I. Title.
HD1379.E35 1998
333.333'83—dc20   93-14445
CIP

Workman Publishing
708 Broadway
New York, NY 10003-9555

Printed in the United States of America
First printing May 1998
10 9 8 7 6

Publisher's Note

This book does not provide legal opinions or advice and does not substitute for the advice of counsel in assessing and minimizing legal risks in the sale of your home. Readers are directed to the "Transferring Ownership" section on page 203. A professional familiar with the laws affecting the sale of real estate in your state should be consulted before implementing the methods suggested.

Contents

A True Story

In 1991 I had a home in Stamford, Connecticut, that was costing me $3,000 a month to maintain.

When I asked my broker to sell it, he said the market was so bad I should wait six months. Six months and $18,000 later, he told me the market was even worse and I'd better wait another six months.

But I couldn't wait another six months! That home was eating me alive and I didn't know what to do.

I decided to run an ad just like the one on the front cover of this book (except the price in my ad was $255,000). I received over 100 telephone calls, and more than 40 families came to visit my home during the two days it was open for inspection.

Five days after placing the ad, I sold my home for $271,500! I got $16,500 more than I asked and $50,000 more than my broker thought he could get. I saved $18,000 in interest and taxes, and I didn't have to pay a $16,290 commission.

I put $84,290 more into my pocket than I would have if I had followed my broker's advice.

Another True Story

I'm often asked how I came to write this book. I'm just a computer guy. I'm not a professional author and I'm not a real estate person.

Six months after selling my home in five days I went to a college reunion. There, I bumped into the shortstop from my intramural baseball team, whom I hadn't seen in 25 years. Not knowing exactly what to say, I said, "Hi, Alan, how're you earning a living?"

He said, "I'm a book agent. I specialize in how-to's."

At first I didn't understand what he meant. Then suddenly I got it.

"Oh," I said, "something like 'How to Sell Your Home in Five Days'?"

He squinted his eyes and said, "Do you know how to do that?"

I told him the true story I've recounted on the previous page, and we spent the rest of the reunion talking about selling homes in five days.

"You've got to write that book," he said. "I'm sure I can sell it. Just send me an outline."

When I got home I simply forgot about the conversation. I enjoyed talking to Alan, but as far as I was concerned it was just "party talk."

Four months later Alan called. "Where's the book?" he asked.

"There's no book," I said, "there's just a seven-line classified ad in *The New York Times*."

He begged me to spend just enough time on it so he could sell it to a publisher.

He was so sure of himself, and I was so flattered, I did it.

Alan sold the book in 5 days using the 5-Day Method.

The rest is history.

The 5-Day Method

```
┌─────────────────────────────────────────────┐
│ PLACENTIA                         BY OWNER    │
│ 4 BR   3 Bath   2,200 Sq. Ft.   Open Kitchen  │
│       Central Air   Cathedral Ceilings        │
│       $199,500 or Best Reasonable Offer       │
│          Inspection Sat.–Sun. 10–5            │
│       Home will be sold Sunday Night to       │
│ HIGHEST BIDDER            (608) 555-3138      │
└─────────────────────────────────────────────┘
```

1. Run an ad like this in the classified "Homes for Sale" section of your newspaper.
2. Answer the telephone.
3. Show your home on Saturday and Sunday from 10 A.M. until 5 P.M.
4. Sell your home Sunday night to the highest bidder.

That's all there is to it.

This book explains how the process works, why it works, and what you must do to make it work for you. The simple ad shown above is the key to selling your home in five days. If you follow the plan outlined in this book, you'll sell your home in five days and receive the highest possible price.

SOUNDS
TOO GOOD
TO BE TRUE

It's Not a Trick

I know the 5-Day Method sounds too good to be true, but it's not a trick.

Thousands of people all over the county have sold their homes in five days after reading this book. They advertise when they think the time is right. They answer the phone when it's convenient for them. They show their home when the house looks its best. They sell quickly. They make more money than they could any other way. They move when they're ready. They get their money when they need it. They take no risk.

The 5-Day Method has been used in rising markets, stagnant markets, and falling markets. It's been used on homes ranging in value from less than $10,000 to several million dollars. It's been used in cities, suburbs, and rural areas. It's been used on freestanding homes, semidetached homes, multi-family homes, and trailer homes; row houses, town houses, apartments, co-ops, condos, boathouses...you name it.

Anyone can do it.

A Better Way to Sell Your Home

Selling your home using the conventional method is a nightmare. You've got to keep everything spotless 24 hours a day, 7 days a week, because brokers can bring buyers at any time. You've got to hide your valuables because potential buyers sometimes turn out to be thieves looking for homes to target.

If you're at home when buyers arrive, the broker may ask you to leave. If you're away, there's a locked box on your door with a key inside so they can enter.

You never know if someone has gone through your home while you were out. You can't say when it will be sold. You have no idea how much you'll get.

You may be forced to buy a new home before you've sold the old one, or you may be forced out of your old home before you buy a new one. Some family members may have to move to a new location while others stay behind.

You know you'll move, but you don't know when. Your life is on hold while you wait. Its maddening, and it can go on for years.

Adding insult to injury, you'll pay thousands of dollars more for using this inferior method.

The 5-Day Method is a better way to sell a home.

Faster

No one will guarantee they'll sell your home for you in less than a week. But you can sell it yourself in just five days if you use this method. This is the fastest way to sell your home.

Now, when I say you'll sell your home in five days, I mean you'll sell your home in exactly five days, not four, not six.

The 5-Day sale always runs on the same five days of the week—Wednesday through Sunday.

Wednesday, Thursday, and Friday are your safety valve. You run your open house on Saturday and Sunday. On Sunday night you sell your home—exactly five days after your ad first appeared in the newspaper.

In five days it's all over!

More Profitable

Just because you sell your home fast, don't think you'll sell it cheap. The 5-Day Method will get you the top end of the fair market value for your home.

I've spoken with hundreds of people who had homes on the market for years before trying the 5-Day Method. In five days they got more money for their homes than they'd ever been offered using the conventional method.

The 5-Day Method works because the free market system works. The market will always drive the price to the highest possible level! What's more, you pay no commission when you use the 5-Day Method, and you'll save thousands of dollars in interest and taxes by selling your home immediately.

You'll get a higher price and put more money in your pocket using the 5-Day Method than you will any other way.

No Risk

There's NO RISK when you sell your home using the 5-Day Method as long as you adhere to the following rule:

IF YOU FAIL TO GET 25 CALLS BY FRIDAY NIGHT YOU STOP THE SALE!

This is an absolute rule. It's your safety valve. It's built into the system and it will always protect you. I'll repeat this rule many times throughout this book because it's so important. *Follow this rule and there is no risk.*

If you get fewer than 25 calls by Friday night, you telephone everyone who responded to your ad and explain you've postponed the sale but you will reschedule and let them know when you do.

Then figure out what went wrong.

(Hint: In 99.9% of all cases the starting price was too high.)

If you do get 25 calls by Friday night, you can proceed without risk. Your sale will closely follow this book. You'll get between 75 and 100 calls by Sunday night. More than 40 buyers will come through your home during your two-day inspection.

You'll sell your home in five days at the highest possible price.

Works Every Time

Suppose you had a $100 bill you wanted to sell.

To get your business currency, brokers might say that they could get you $110 for your $100 bill.

Of course, that's not true, no one would pay $110 for a $100 bill. So, a few months later, your broker would suggest you drop the price to $100. Still, no one would bite. Why should they? $100 for a $100 bill is not a good deal.

Then your broker would tell you to drop the price to $95. Immediately someone would snap up that $100 bill. Your broker would take a $6 commission and give you $89.

Now if you decided to sell your $100 bill yourself, using the 5-Day Method, you'd take it into a bar or any other place with 30 or 40 people and announce you'll sell your $100 bill for $50 or the best offer you got in the next five minutes.

Someone would ask if you'd *really* take $50 for the $100 bill. You'd immediately answer if that's the best offer you get, you'll take it. The questioner would offer you $50. Someone else would say $55. The price would quickly move to between $95 and $100 because $99.50 for a $100 bill is still a good deal. In less than five minutes you'd sell that bill for more than a broker would get you in months of trying.

Selling your home using the 5-Day Method works exactly the same way.

If you follow this book, price your home properly, and attract a sufficient number of interested buyers, you'll sell your home for its fair market price. Interested buyers will not permit other buyers to purchase your home for less than they are willing to pay for it. They'll bid the price up to the fair market value just as surely as strangers in a crowd will vie for a bargain on a $100 bill.

The 5-Day Method works every time because everyone wants a bargain.

BROKER HOKUM

Who Are These People?

Before stumbling across the 5-Day Method I always relied on real estate brokers.

Not anymore.

There are more than half a million real estate brokers in the United States. Most sell a home or two, then decide they'll never make a living at it and move on. Few of these people have any more experience selling homes than you do, and considerably less than I do.

Your home is probably your most valuable asset. Selling it for the right amount is the best way to ensure your financial future. It's crazy to entrust your most important asset to a part-timer when you can do it better yourself. If you use the 5-Day Method you'll do a better job than anyone can do for you.

Beware of false expertise.

What Are They Worth?

The average real estate commission is $7,500.

If you sell your home the conventional way, you must sign a contract that obligates you to pay a percentage of the selling price to the broker if your home is sold during a certain time period. If the broker finds a buyer willing to pay your price, you must pay the commission even if you don't take the deal. If you find a buyer yourself during that time period, you still must pay the commission. Once brokers have signed you to a contract it's of little concern to them if your home remains unsold because the asking price is too high. You're locked in for the entire period of the contract and there's nothing you can do about it.

On the other hand, what if the broker sells your home in one day? That's probably even worse. You've sold your home too cheaply! The very first person who walked through the door knew you were offering your home for less than it was worth. That's a disaster for you. Not only did you sell too cheap, you must also pay a commission for getting bad advice.

When you use the 5-Day Method you're not locked into the price you list in your ad. If your home is worth more, you'll get more.

The average cost of running a 5-Day sale is $500.

Why would you pay someone $7,500 to do something you can do better, for $500?

The Pricing Bait and Switch

When the time comes to price your home, many brokers will tell you what you want to hear because they know you can't hold them to what they say, while they can hold you to their contract.

"Wow," you say. "This broker will get me more money for my home than anyone else—this is the broker for me—where do I sign?"

This is a prescription for disaster.

The contract you sign with your broker ties you up far longer and in more ways than you may realize.

The broker has no obligation to get you the quoted price, but you have an obligation to pay the broker during the contract period regardless of who actually sells your home or what price it actually commands. If you sell your home after the contract period to a buyer originally brought in by your broker, you still must pay the broker's fee.

You can't fool the market. You won't flush out unrealistically high bids by asking unrealistically high prices. After your home has been on the market at a ridiculously high price for three months, or six months, or nine months, and nobody has come to see it (with the possible exception of the broker's cousin), either you or your broker will suggest dropping the price.

By then you'll be desperate. Your home will be dragging you down. You'll have to get rid of it. You'll no longer care what you get for it, as long as you can put an end to the monthly payments. Just stopping the pain will feel good!

So you'll drop the price. Buyers will realize your home has been on the market for months and you're in trouble. Other brokers will steer their clients to your home because you're selling cheap. You'll be offered even less than you're now asking. But that'll be the first offer you'll get. You'll want to sell before the price goes down even further. You'll have no choice. You'll sell.

The broker who got you in trouble with the silly selling price will still make out like a bandit!

I can't tell you how to select a broker, but I can tell you how *not* to select one. Stay away from brokers who talk about impossible prices if you sign exclusive deals with them.

Don't fall for the pricing bait and switch.

A Conflict of Interest

Your broker has a built-in conflict of interest. Brokers make money only if your home is sold. A bad deal for you can be a great deal for your broker.

Let's say your broker spends a year trying to get $100,000 for your home without success. Your broker's contract will soon expire. The broker then finds someone willing to pay $90,000 and tries to talk you into accepting it.

What's going on here?

The broker's commission on $100,000 is $6,000. If your broker talks you into accepting $90,000, the commission is $5,400. That's a difference to the broker of only $600. Your broker gets nothing if the contract expires without a sale.

Of course, your broker will push you very hard to accept this offer, even though it may not be in your best interest. If you accept the offer you'll put $84,600 in your pocket instead of the $100,000 you were told you could expect.

If you run a 5-Day sale and the best offer is only $90,000, you'll still put $89,500 in your pocket (after the $500 cost of running a 5-Day sale). That's $4,900 more than getting the same price through a broker. I don't know about you, but for me, $4,900 is enough to care about.

Compounding this problem is the practice of real estate brokers who buy homes directly from sellers. How can a broker represent the seller's best interests when the broker is also the buyer? Many brokers then take another

6% out of the sale price for their commission.

Even if you think your broker is your "friend," it's important to understand that brokers act in their own best interests. If you're lucky, your interests will overlap theirs.

Don't "Protect the Broker"

Real estate brokers who see your ad will know you're offering your home at a great price. They'll want to bring their clients to see it. They'll ask you to pay them a commission if their client buys your home. This is called "protecting the broker."

Don't do it!

You'll get the top price without the help of any broker. Don't pay a commission when you don't have to.

Instead, tell the broker to bid on behalf of the client with the understanding that the buyer, not you, will pay the broker's fee in the event of a sale. Tell the broker whatever the buyer bids is the amount you get. The broker and the buyer can make their own deal, and you don't want to know what it is.

This allows you to treat the broker's client like any other buyer. This allows you to treat all bids the same way. It's both clear and equitable to all involved. No one has an advantage. Everyone pays the same.

THE BUYER POOL

Jump In

At any given time, only a certain number of buyers will be interested in a home like yours in a location like yours at a price like yours. This group of buyers is called the "buyer pool" for your home. The participants constantly change as some buyers purchase homes, some get frustrated and leave the pool, and others make the decision to buy and enter the pool.

Many sellers make the mistake of restricting the size of their buyer pool by pricing their homes too high. They expect to be offered less than the asking price, so they raise their price to get a higher bid.

Few home buyers are experienced. Most are dimly aware that some home sellers may accept less than the asking price, but they don't know how much less. They see a certain price and say, "We can't afford that—let's not even bother to look." When this happens, the seller has decreased the size of the buyer pool. Some buyers who shut themselves out of the pool may have been prepared to offer more than the amount finally accepted, but the seller will never know. *This results in a lower selling price for your home.*

When you use the 5-Day Method, you offer your home for less than you think you'll actually get in order to attract more buyers, who will bid against one another for the privilege of buying your home. *This results in a higer selling price for your home.*

The 5-Day Method allows you to make a big splash in the buyer pool. You must make sure your ad is seen by virtually everyone looking for a home like yours. If enough buyers respond, you'll sell your home in five days, for the highest possible price.

The Three Real Buyers

No matter what method you use to sell your home, there are only three real buyers.

Well, maybe it's two, and maybe it's four, but please understand that out of the hundreds of people who may say they're interested in your home, most neither can afford it nor will want to buy it. At any given time there's just a small number of buyers who are actually willing and able to take real money out of their pockets and give it to you.

When you run a 5-Day sale, your job is to make sure the entire buyer pool for your home shows up for the sale. Hiding somewhere inside that buyer pool are those three real buyers. You may not be able to spot them in the crowd, but you must make sure they all participate.

The easiest way to accomplish this is to advertise a very low starting price. The real buyers will know the real value of your home. Because your starting price is low they may think there's something wrong. Or they may think you simply don't know what your home is worth. In either case they've got to make a phone call to find out what's going on. After you describe your home they'll come to your Open House. After they see your home, they'll bid.

This is the nature of a 5-Day sale. It's the reason you start low. It doesn't matter that most of the people who inspect your home are not real buyers. It doesn't matter that many of the people who come can't afford your home. It doesn't matter if your starting price is half what you're hoping for. The only thing that really matters is that the three real buyers come to your sale and bid.

Don't "Qualify" Them

Real estate brokers seek to "qualify" buyers. This means they try to determine what each buyer can actually afford. They won't waste their time showing homes to buyers who lack the means to pay for them.

When you use the 5-Day Method there's no need to qualify buyers. You wind up with so many people inspecting your home you don't have time to figure out who's qualified and who's not. People who can afford your home may change their minds at the last minute. People who can't afford it may find a way if they want it badly enough.

Buyers understand there's no point bidding more than they can pay. You're not going to renegotiate; you'll simply drop down to the next bidder. The buyers sort themselves out without any help from you, and the top bidder almost always has the money.

The only buyer you must qualify is the top bidder, and your settlement agent will do that for you.

As far as you're concerned, the speed with which you conduct the sale separates the qualified buyers from the unqualified buyers. If the top bidder is unable to come up with the money, you immediately drop down to the next bidder. The only truly qualified buyer is one whose money is in your hands. Everyone else is a maybe.

End-Buyers

When you think of selling your home you're probably thinking of selling it to an end-buyer—the next person who will actually live in your home.

In most cases this is true. If your home is in decent shape, and you run your 5-Day sale properly, you'll get the top end of the fair market price. Professionals won't be able to buy your home cheap, then turn around and sell it at a profit to someone else.

You will probably be more comfortable with end-buyers. They are easier to deal with than professionals because they know as much about buying and selling homes as you do. They will stumble around and do their best, just like you.

You will both recognize that neither of you is a professional. This will help you to trust each other, and will make any attempt to cheat or weasel more obvious to the other. Neither of you knows enough to be a good cheat.

Most of the buyers you will see will be end-buyers, and most likely you will sell your home to one of them.

Professional Buyers

Because your starting price is so far below market value you should expect to see a lot of professional buyers.

Professional buyers include real estate brokers looking for homes to buy under market value; builders planning to remodel and resell homes; speculators planning to "flip" homes (buy cheaply then quickly resell at a profit); and developers planning to buy properties strictly for the value of the land.

Don't be afraid of professional buyers. By their presence they validate your starting price. If you don't see professional buyers, you didn't start low enough.

Sometimes professional buyers will pay more for your home than anyone else. If your home is not pretty, or is substantially damaged, it may be worth more to professional buyers than to end-buyers. The fact that you can attract scores of interested prospects, even in its current condition, will add value in the minds of professional buyers. They are willing to spend money to improve your home to make a profit.

Professional buyers are not shy about leaving bids. They understand better than end-buyers do the value of your home. They will leave high bids early to scare off other bidders. They are professionals and they don't have time to fool around. Their bids are good for you and great for them.

If there are many buyers for your home, the professional buyers will push up the price until it approaches the retail level, and then leave end-buyers to fight it out.

If, for some reason, all end-buyers drop out of the bidding, professional buyers will remain. They provide you with a floor. They'll be there to buy your home if they can buy it at their price or on their terms. In balance, they're very good for you.

Please note, professionals can fix your home for less than you can. Sometimes they lose money when they resell. Don't think that you can compete with them. If they are the high bidder, sell them the house and don't think twice about it.

Cash Buyers

You may want to give a discount to people who can pay cash. There are surprisingly many of them. Some have just sold their homes. Others may have parents who can put up cash while they apply for a mortgage. Then there are those with cash businesses who may have difficulty obtaining a mortgage but have plenty of cash on hand.

If the buyer pays cash, you don't need the approval of a third party to conclude your sale. There are no mortgage commitments to worry about.

Cash deals are fast deals, but that might not be important to you. Cash deals are sure deals, but you may have mortgage buyers willing to pay much more. Speed and certainty may not be worth anything extra to you, but if all other things are equal, cash deals are preferable.

If you are offering a cash discount, pick an amount, not a percentage. Amounts are easier to figure and understand

Here's how to figure out what cash is worth: add your mortgage payments for a year to your tax payments for a year, and divide by 365. This tells you how much your home costs you every day.

Multiply the daily cost of your home times the number of days you will allow for your buyer to get a mortgage. (Your settlement agent can help you with this.) The number you come up with is the value of cash. You can expect to put exactly the same amount in your pocket if you give the buyer the cash discount as you would by waiting longer for the higher amount and continuing to pay your mortgage and taxes.

The easiest way to explain a cash discount is to tell everyone if they pay cash they can give you $5,000 (or whatever amount you pick) less than the amount they bid. I've found everyone can understand this, they can easily factor it in while bidding, and everyone knows they've been offered the same deal.

Mortgage Buyers

The majority of people can't buy a home with cash. They must go to a bank and borrow most of the money. The bank will check out their financial health to establish their ability to repay the loan. Then the bank will want to look at the home to make certain it's worth more than the amount to be borrowed. These procedures may take from days to months.

In most cases, if the buyer is unable to get a mortgage within a given period, the sale can be voided by either party, and you may have to sell your home all over again.

"Prequalified" mortgage buyers are buyers who have already started the mortgage process. They went to the bank before they started looking for a home. They have already filled out the financial forms and the bank has told them how much they are qualified to borrow.

"Preapproved" mortgage buyers have actually submitted an application for a loan to a bank and paid all the fees. They are all set to buy a home worth up to a certain amount, provided the bank's appraiser agrees the home is worth the more than the loan.

Your home is the collateral for a mortgage loan. The bank will want to take a look at it to make sure it's worth what the buyer has offered to pay. Neither you nor the buyer has any control over this process. Sometimes the bank will not give a preapproved buyer enough money to buy your home.

Anticipate that it will take 30 to 60 days for most people to get a mortgage, even if the bank knows the buyer and has already authorized the loan.

NOW IS
THE TIME

Are You Really Ready?

This sounds like a rhetorical question, but it's not. The 5-Day Method works so fast, it's over almost before it begins. The process is radically different from the conventional method primarily because it's designed to happen quickly. You must *really* be ready before you start. This book demystifies a simple process. Ordinary people all over the country have used it and sold their homes in five days. You can too!

Traditionally, people who don't have to move start by saying they would sell their home if someone came along who offered them more money than they think it's worth. With sugarplums dancing in their heads, they locate a real estate broker and "list" their home at an inflated price. They haven't even begun to think seriously about moving, because no serious buyer would pay the price they're asking. People using this method are fully prepared to sit around for months, or years, knowing it's unlikely they will ever sell their home at the listed price.

The 5-Day Method works the other way around. It unites a buyer who is ready to buy with a seller who is ready to sell. The buyer and the seller work together to achieve their common goal. Everyone else is forced out of the middle until a final price is negotiated. Only then are professionals brought in to conclude the financial and legal aspects in the conventional way.

If you're really ready to sell, after reading and absorbing this book in its entirety, you'll spend a total of five days engaged in very intense work. By the end of the five days, you will have located a buyer and sold your home.

If you're not really ready, don't start.

Furnished or Empty?

It doesn't seem to matter to buyers whether your home is furnished or empty, although individual buyers may have a preference one way or the other.

If you have valuable antiques on display, some buyers may overlook flaws in your home because they're concentrating on your beautiful things. Other buyers, not liking your taste, may be distracted by your possessions and overlook good points in the house itself. Most buyers are sophisticated enough to be able to see past the furniture or to be able to envision their furniture in your empty home.

From your perspective, it's simpler to sell your home empty. You don't have to worry about breakage or pilferage. If there is nothing to damage or steal, you can concentrate on the primary job of selling your home.

If you have a choice, pick the easy way: empty most of your home before you sell it. Take out all the knickknacks. Remove anything you care about and everything that can be broken. Empty the closets and drawers. Leave only large pieces of furniture and enough tables and chairs so you can be comfortable during the sale.

The rest of us will just have to sell our homes as they are, and remain more vigilant while strangers are going through our things.

Either way, it won't change the final price you receive for your home.

Pick a Day— Any Day

I'm sure you've been told springtime is the best time to sell a home. More buyers look for homes in the spring, and more homes are sold in the spring. But springtime may not be the best time for you. When you use the 5-Day Method you can successfully sell your home at any time of year. The 5-Day Method works just as well in the dead of winter as in the most glorious spring.

I know of homeowners in Mt. Kisco, New York, who moved to New Mexico for health reasons before they could sell their home. The home was gorgeous and had been featured in *Architectural Digest.* One of its outstanding features was a Japanese bonsai garden. The homeowners tried to sell their home, using the conventional method, for two years.

They stumbled across the 5-Day Method in the middle of a severe Northeast winter just as their contract with the latest in a succession of brokers was about to expire. They decided to give it a try.

Callers responding to their ad had to call New Mexico. Friends would handle their open house. How could they know a blizzard would strike on Friday night? More than two feet of snow fell. The beautiful bonsai garden was buried under the snow.

By the time their friends arrived with a snowplow, there were eight buyers waiting at the bottom of the driveway. The home was sold for exactly the price they wanted in five days.

Remember, there are disadvantages as well as advantages to selling in the spring. There are many more homes on the market, and more ads in the newspaper competing with yours. Buyers have more homes to look at, so they may not get to yours. It's harder to know if the three real buyers inspected and bid on your home. More important, you may need to sell your home at some other time of year.

Forget about trying to sell your home at a time you think will be good for buyers. When you use the 5-Day Method, you can sell your home *whenever* it's good for you.

Lead Time

How much lead time you need is up to you.

I've spoken with people who bought this book on a Monday and sold their home the following Sunday. You can't sell your home much faster than that, but that's an extreme example and I wouldn't recommend it.

Most people allow themselves a little more time and probably make a little more money because they do. Unless you plan major renovations, you should be able to run your 5-Day sale within a month of reading this book.

No matter when you run your sale, be sure to use the checklist in the back of the book (pages 251–252). It lists every step and tells you where to look if you don't understand something.

I still use the checklist myself, even though I've run hundreds of 5-Day sales. Sometimes I forget something. When I use the checklist I find what I forgot before it trips me up.

Bad Times

Although you can run your 5-Day sale at any time of year, there are certain weeks that won't work as well as others. You should avoid three-day weekends, major religious holidays, big sporting events, and any other days that might be particularly inconvenient for buyers. People will turn their schedules upside down to get to your sale, but they can't skip Christmas with their mother in Minnesota.

If you run your sale at a bad time you may still get a healthy turnout, but one or more of the real buyers may not attend. Those who do come will correctly conclude other buyers won't show up, and they'll be able to buy your home for less. Don't let this happen!

Don't plan your sale for Christmas, New Year's Day, or Easter. Don't conduct the sale over any of the three-day weekends—Martin Luther King Day; Presidents Day; Memorial Day; Labor Day. Avoid Mother's Day, Father's Day, Thanksgiving week, and the Fourth of July week. Stay away from Super Bowl Sunday.

If you anticipate buyers from specific ethnic groups, check out their holidays and celebrations and don't schedule your sale when it will create a conflict for them. If you know a hurricane, blizzard, or flood is heading your way, wait until after it passes to conduct your sale.

WHAT TO FIX

Start with a Radon Test

The very first thing to do is a radon test. Radon tests take longer to perform than anything else you must do, and the longer the test, the more accurate the results. High radon levels are easily corrected, but if you discover a radon problem you'll have to retest your home after fixing it. Do the radon test right away.

Radon testing is a simple, inexpensive process you can do yourself. Buy a radon kit at your local hardware store. Don't worry—they're made for people who've never used them before. Follow the instructions carefully, ventilating the test area beforehand in accordance with the manufacturer's directions. Run the longest test possible, then send the canister to the lab for evaluation. You should have the results within two weeks.

If your radon count is too high, fix it. Then retest. This could take another two weeks. Always provide results of your radon tests to your prospective buyers.

Have Your Home Inspected by a Pro

Before starting work on your home, you must understand what does and doesn't need to be fixed. Have your home inspected by an independent home inspection company. In some states such an inspection is required before a home can be sold, but have one done whether it's required or not.

Professional home inspectors will tell you more about your home than you ever knew. You'll wonder why you didn't have it inspected before. The report will describe your home in all its technical aspects, tell you what things require immediate repair, and what things will require attention over a longer period of time. The report helps you figure out what to do next.

Look at a sample report from the company before you contract for the inspection. Make sure you are satisfied with the way it looks because you will show the inspection report to others. It should look as good as everything else in your home. Hand-written inspection reports, fill-in-the-blanks, and checkboxes may be just as accurate as typed or computer-generated reports, but they don't look as good. Select a company that will give you a professional-looking report.

If you have a well, have it tested. If you have a septic system, have a percolation test performed. If repairs must be made, you can either make them yourself or disclose them before they pop up and kill your sale.

If you fix things after your home is inspected, indicate them on the report. Show the inspection report to all prospective buyers. This will eliminate surprises that could come up later. After the bidding, buyers can confirm that the inspection company is reputable, that the inspector will stand behind the report, and that all repairs have been made properly.

By conducting these tests in advance, you answer buyers' questions and reduce the time it takes to close the sale. Because you disclose all tests prior to the bidding, test results will not cause a renegotiation at the settlement. Since you've paid for tests often not performed by sellers, your home is even more desirable to buyers, who will save money and know what they're getting before they start bidding.

Inspect It Yourself

After you know what the professionals think about your home, you must honestly evaluate it yourself. Pretend you're a buyer. Apart from the things that *must* be fixed, what things would you *want* fixed?

If your kitchen is so sad you want to cry every time you enter it, think about some changes. In terms of the initial impression your home makes, the kitchen is the most important room. A good kitchen can sell a mediocre home. Forget about major changes. You'll never get back what you spend. Sometimes simply refacing the counters and cabinets and replacing knobs can turn a disaster into a perfectly acceptable kitchen.

Look at your bathrooms. After kitchens, they're the next room checked out by buyers. Here again, don't go crazy. Don't spend money you'll never recover. Clean everything. Fixtures can be replaced at a nominal cost. At the very least, make sure the existing fixtures don't leak.

Do something about the garage and the attic. If you have a garage door opener, make sure it works smoothly. If not, take it out. You're better off without an opener than with one you must constantly apologize for.

Bring in contractors. Ask them what they think should be fixed. Show them your independent inspection report. Some contractors specialize in preparing homes for sale. They know how to get the best results for the least money.

With contractors' suggestions and the home inspection report in hand, you're in a good position to decide what to fix and what not to fix.

The Fix-It Rule of Thumb

Knowing what to fix is surprisingly simple because there's a surprisingly simple rule of thumb:

Fix nothing unless you're certain you'll get back two dollars for every dollar you spend.

(Hint: That's almost never the case.)

There are just three categories of things you should even consider fixing:

1. Legally required things
2. Little things that make a big difference
3. Big things that make a huge difference

Legally you've got no choice on some things. You've got to fix certain things because that's the law. Often these are environmental matters, or hidden hazards particularly harmful to children. Examples are lead paint and asbestos removal. Some laws are national, others are local. Your settlement agent will tell you which apply to you.

Little things that make a big difference are all those things you always planned to fix and never got around to. If you don't already have a list of them, make one. Fix everything on the list. When people inspect your home they may see one or two major projects that need fixing, but not dozens of little things.

Some examples of little things that make a big difference are:

1. Replacing all the old doorknobs and plates that cover the light

switches and electrical outlets

2. Fixing all leaky faucets, damaged trim, doors that don't close properly, broken screens, rain gutters, etc.

3. Cleaning clutter wherever you see it

These are little things. You know what they are because they've been bothering you. Don't let them bother your buyers. You can fix them quickly and easily, and you'll certainly get back two dollars for every dollar you spend on these annoying little problems.

Apart from what's legally required, and the little annoyances such as switch plates and leaky faucets, it rarely pays to fix anything else. Generally speaking, fixing big things will enrich contractors and the buyer at your expense. Big things cost a lot of money, take a lot of time, and won't return two dollars for every dollar you spend.

Don't kid yourself. Fix only those things that meet the fix-it rule of thumb.

When in Doubt, Don't Fix It

Many homeowners waste a lot of time and money fixing things better left alone. Buyers might hate the work you've just done. They may prefer to pay less now and make renovations to their own specifications at a later time, when they can better afford it. Some will be able to do the work for less than it cost you.

Add up the cost of everything you think you should fix before you start. You may discover you plan to do $50,000 worth of repairs on a home you hope will sell for $125,000. I can guarantee you're better off selling your home for $75,000 as is, rather than spending the $50,000 and hoping to sell it at the absolute top end of the market for $125,000—and netting the same $75,000, if you're lucky.

One homeowner told me about selling his home after spending $50,000 remodeling the kitchen. He went back to see his old home a month after the settlement only to find the new buyer had demolished the old house, new kitchen and all. The new kitchen had made no difference to the buyer, who was interested only in the land. The seller had thrown out $50,000. He would have received the exact same price without the new kitchen.

Make repairs only if you are *sure* every dollar you spend will bring back two dollars when you sell. When in doubt, don't fix it!

THE
STARTING
PRICE

5-Day Pricing Is Easy

When you use the conventional method, pricing is the hardest part. If you price your home too low, you sell it too cheap; if you price too high, you don't sell it at all. A little mistake can cost you a lot of money.

When you use the 5-Day Method, pricing is easy. You never have to guess what your home is worth because the price you put in your ad is just the starting price. It's neither the most you can hope for, nor the least you'll take.

YOU CAN'T PRICE YOUR HOME TOO LOW!

If your starting price is very low, you may get 100 calls by Friday night. That will make you work harder, but it won't change the selling price. If your starting price is too high, you won't get 25 calls by Friday night. Then you must stop your sale and start again another weekend, using a lower starting price.

Clearly, you're better off starting a 5-Day sale too low rather than starting too high, but neither mistake is fatal. You'll still sell your home. You'll still get the highest possible price. The starting price simply isn't critical. It's just a number you put in your ad. It's designed to do just one thing: get you a minimum of 25 calls by Friday night. That's all.

Ballpark Pricing

Before you can begin the process of establishing a specific price for your home, you must establish some sort of broad range. This is often called "ballpark pricing."

You know that if you offered your home for $50 you could sell it in ten minutes. You know that if you offered your home for $50 million you would never sell it. The right price for your home is somewhere between $50 and $50 million.

Now you have to narrow it down. You already know the value of your home is closer to $50 than to $50 million. But what is it exactly?

Let's say you own the average American home. To begin with, you know it's certainly worth more than $10,000; more than $25,000; more than $50,000; yes, certainly it's worth more than $75,000. You *know* that if you offered to sell your home for $75,000 you'd have to fight off the buyers. On the low end, you *know for sure* your home is worth more than $75,000. But how much more?

Now work on the problem from the high end. A $50 million price is ridiculous. So is $1 million, and $500,000, and $250,000. You know your home won't bring $200,000. Maybe it could have brought $150,000 at the height of the market, but you know you can't get that now.

The truth is, in today's market you'd be happy to get $120,000 for your home, and you'd be thrilled to get $125,000. So your true ballpark range works out to be somewhere between $75,000 and $125,000.

Your starting price should be $25,000 to $50,000 below the bottom end of your ballpark price. In this example your starting price would be $49,500. At that price you *know* your phone will ring off the hook. You *know* people will flock to see your home. You *know* you'll sell your home in five days.

Magic Numbers

The starting price should always be a magic number.

"What's a magic number?" you may well ask.

We've all seen magic numbers, and they've worked their magic on all of us. "$9.95" is a magic number.

"Oh, come on," you'll say, "I hate prices like that. That's really ten dollars. You can't fool me."

But these numbers *do* fool us: $9.95 will outsell $10 every day of the week. In our hearts we call $9.95 "nine bucks" and $10.00 "ten bucks." Don't fight human nature. The starting price for your home should always be a magic number.

Magic numbers are also useful because they are less likely to look like misprints. If you use a round number like $25,000 people may think you intended $250,000. They may even insert the extra 0 in their minds. If that number was $24,500 most people would correctly interpret the price.

Unless a home is worth less than $25,000, prices in 5-Day ads should always end with $24,500; $49,500; $74,500; or $99,500. Every buyer recognizes these as magic numbers, and that's what you want. Don't try to fine-tune these prices. Don't use oddball prices that make people think! Use easily understood magic numbers that make people call to find out what's going on.

5-Day Pricing

Here's the 5-Day pricing rule of thumb:

Ask what the buyer wants to pay, not what you hope to receive.

If your ballpark price is $100,000 and you start your home at $99,500, you can't expect 25 calls by Friday night. While $99,500 may be a fair price, it's not a great price. It won't bring the buyers out of the woodwork. It doesn't shout "THIS HOME WILL BE SOLD SUNDAY NIGHT."

Your starting price should always be at least $25,000 below your ballpark price. To be on the safe side, I usually start at least $50,000 below the ballpark price. The starting price on a $100,000 home should be either $74,500 or $49,500.

I would always pick $49,500 because I know I will attract all the real buyers at that price. If your home is *really* worth $100,000 you'll probably do all right at $74,500. But if you start at $49,500 you'll get 25 calls by Friday night, even if your home isn't worth $100,000. That's why I would always start at $49,500. With very expensive homes I've started as much as $500,000 below the ballpark price.

Don't get emotional about the starting price. You won't receive the price you show in your ad. The market determines the fair price for every home offered for sale.

To select your starting price you must answer just one question:

"Will this price will get me 25 calls by Friday night?"

If you're not sure, drop the price by $25,000 and ask the question again. Keep asking and dropping the price until you are *positive* you'll get at least 25 calls by Friday night.

Now try your price on friends and family. Do they tell you you're crazy? Do they say if the house sells for that price they want to buy it? Are *they* certain you'll get more than 25 calls by Friday night? Don't place your ad until everyone you ask agrees you've arrived at an irresistible starting price.

There is no financial penalty for starting your price too low.

PUT IT IN WRITING

"You're So Organized!"

One of the things you'll hear over and over during your sale is the remark, "You're so organized!" When you run a 5-Day sale it's easy to be organized. You know exactly when people are coming. You know exactly what questions they'll ask. You're ready for them.

Between Wednesday and Sunday you'll get over 100 telephone calls. More than 40 families should visit during your Open House. Any of these people could turn out to be one of the three real buyers, so you must be sure everyone gets the right information. The easiest way to do this is to write it down and print it up before the sale begins, while your head is clear.

At a minimum, printed information should include:

- A Quick Description
- A Detailed Description
- An Independent Inspection Report
- The Bidding Method and rules

Assembling this information ahead of time will allow you and others in your household to field all questions from callers simply by referring to the printed sheets. Potential buyers who come to see your home will have most of the answers right at their fingertips.

Write the information exactly the way you want to present it over the phone. Use a separate sheet of paper for each topic and insert a copy of your ad at the top of each page. Make at least 100 copies of each information sheet, using a different color paper for each.

Staple together a complete information packet and leave it beside each telephone in your home. Keep the remainder of the pages loose so you can set them out, in separate piles, one topic to a pile, for the inspection.

Your information sheets will save you a lot of time and trouble. They will reinforce your ad, your home, and your sale in the minds of all buyers. More important, by writing it all down you can be sure everyone gets the same information.

Quick Description

Think of the Quick Description as the ad you wanted to put into the newspaper, but couldn't afford.

The Quick Description should tell the story of your home. It's designed to give prospective buyers enough information so they can decide if they want to know more. When prospective buyers call, whoever answers the phone reads the Quick Description to them.

The Quick Description is your first chance to really sell your home. The newspaper ad is designed to get the calls. Now you can entice buyers.

If you get 100 calls, you don't really want 100 families coming to the inspection. You won't be able to spend enough time with any of them. You know, out of all the callers, only three are real buyers. If 40 potential buyers inspect your home, you can be sure the three real buyers will be in the pack. The Quick Description will help you cull the 40 most likely buyers from the 100 callers.

Write the Quick Description carefully. It should contain the bare minimum every buyer needs to know. Briefly describe the physical features of your home, as well as the property it sits on and its location relative to schools and shopping. Provide figures for yearly property taxes. Repeat the starting price so buyers will know it's not a typographical error. Repeat the inspection times and dates. Briefly explain the bidding process and that your home will be sold Sunday night to the highest bidder.

See Sample Materials, pages 231–232, for a sample Quick Description. Follow the format. Insert your own information and anything else you would want potential buyers to know.

After hearing the Quick Description, some callers will know immediately that your home is not for them and will politely tell you so.

Others will want to hear more.

Detailed Description

Callers who want more details will happily spend as much time on the phone as it takes to make sure they won't be running all over the place, looking at dozens of unsuitable homes. For these callers, the Detailed Description should furnish as much information about your home as you can supply.

If you don't know the correct real estate terms, the proper name for the construction of your home, or some other technical aspect, you'll find this information in the inspection report and in your tax records. Your deed and accompanying maps should answer the legal questions.

Use the Detailed Description to answer all the specific questions about your house, such as roofing; gutter and siding materials; electrical service; water supply and waste method; exact dimensions of every room; and features connected with each room, such as fireplaces and outside access. Appliances that will be left for the buyer should also be listed.

For a sample Detailed Description, see pages 233–234 in the Sample Materials section. Fill in the blanks with information about your home. Eliminate categories that don't apply to you. Add any category you feel is important.

Bidding Method

My Bidding Method sheet is the result of hundreds of sales. It's designed to include as many bidders as possible and it results in the highest possible selling price. Copy it unless you have a very good reason for making changes. It works! You'll find it in the Sample Materials section on page 235.

The Bidding Method sheet explains exactly how the bidding will work. This is the central feature and most unfamiliar aspect of your sale. If prospective buyers understand this sheet, they can easily participate in the process.

Be sure to spell out the entire bidding procedure. Tell when bids may be placed and when the round-robin bidding will begin. Explain how the round-robin will be conducted.

You should review the bidding method with all potential buyers, both over the telephone and when they come to inspect your home.

Directions

Everyone who answers the telephone in your home must be able to give any caller who asks the simplest, easiest-to-follow directions to your home. If you write out a complete set of instructions in advance it will be easy, even for people who feel they're not good at giving directions.

Start from a major road everyone knows. Drive the route yourself before you write it down. Is there a new sign you haven't noticed? Is the billboard that was there for 20 years now gone? Is the big white house now a big blue house?

Check out all distances on your car's odometer. Write out your instructions. Then go out again to try the directions yourself. Make sure you haven't missed a step. Make sure the landmarks given are the same ones you notice when you're driving.

Give every caller the same directions. Don't use shortcuts. Callers who know the area will know the shortcuts. Those who don't know the area will get hopelessly lost. Try to keep instructions short and sweet.

Directions should be printed at the bottom of your Quick Description (see Sample Materials section, pages 231–232).

Full Disclosure

I can't overemphasize the importance of full disclosure.

You must be sure every prospective buyer is bidding on the same home. You must point out every problem. You must point out every potential problem.

If you fail to disclose everything, buyers are certain to discover most, if not all, of the problems before the closing. Buyers may then back out of the deal or demand monetary concessions for problems that you've failed to disclose.

If you disclose everything, buyers can't demand concessions for shortcomings clearly noted in advance. If you have a problem with the high bidder, you can drop to the second bidder, knowing there are no undisclosed problems that could pop up to ruin your sale.

Write the Rules

Your home is your property and you can decide exactly how you want to sell it. It's important to maintain complete control of the 5-Day process. Think this through. You're selling your home in an unconventional way. You must understand what you're doing and how you're doing it well enough to be able to explain it to others.

You write the rules!

Use my rules as the basis for your rules. My rules are proven, easily understood, and designed to obtain the highest possible prices without cheating or taking risks. You may wish to implement other rules, but if you do, check them out with your settlement agent.

Don't try to make up new rules as you go. You'll make mistakes. There will be too many people, and you'll wind up telling different buyers different things. If you are giving a discount for cash, decide what it is beforehand. How and when will you conduct the bidding? How long do you need to move out? Think these things through before you start your sale.

You write the rules for your sale; and you make sure every potential buyer plays by your rules!

Don't make exceptions.

THE
CLASSIFIED
AD

Use My Ad as a Model

Copy my ad.

Not because I wrote the book and I say so.

Copy my ad because you know it works.

My ad has been tested thousands of times. It's clear. It's concise. It does the job. Simply follow my format and substitute your information. If your starting price is low enough and you put the ad in the right places, you'll get over 100 calls.

Don't try to fill in the blanks while you're on the phone talking to the classified ad department. Figure out everything, including how you'll abbreviate words, before you call. Type out your ad or use a word processor to see approximately how it will look on the page.

You don't need a fancy border. You don't need a picture. You don't need a double column. My little seven-line ad works fine just the way it is. Run it for just five days. Any longer is a waste of both time and money.

Every sample ad in this book resulted in a successful 5-Day sale. The ad works. Don't get creative. Stick with the program.

Where to Place It

Your ad will appear for just five days, so you must run it in the right places.

You must place your ad where the three real buyers are sure to see it. To be sure, put it in the two places you would be most likely to look if you were looking for a home in your area. The real buyers will surely look in one if not both of these places. Typically, this means running your ad in one local paper and one regional paper.

If you're not sure, the easiest way to judge a classified section is to see how many home-for-sale ads it carries. If it has a lot, join the crowd. If not, keep looking.

Buyers are lazy, just like you and I are. They don't want to buy three or four newspapers to find homes for sale. They want to be able to pick up a single paper every day and find all the available homes in it. They soon discover ads in smaller classified sections are duplicates of ads found in the larger ones. So they just buy the most popular paper. Make sure your ad is there.

By selecting the top local classified section and the top big-city or regional classified section, you will appeal to prospective buyers who live near you and to those who live somewhere else. People living elsewhere learn the best regional sources for ads and consult them when they look for homes.

It's pointless to advertise in *The Millionaire Times* if your home will sell for $20,000 or to list a multimillion-dollar home in *The Penny Saver*.

Advertise where a reasonable buyer for a home like yours is likely to look.

You don't have to place your ad in every publication within 100 miles of your home. Two well-placed ads will draw the same number of calls as ten ads scattered all over. Put your ad where you can be sure all three real buyers will see it.

I'm frequently asked about placing ads on the Internet. At the present time the Internet is not a good place to advertise a 5-Day sale. This may change in the future, but currently you can't be sure all three real buyers will use the Internet. You can be sure all three buyers will look in the classifieds.

Put your ad where you can be sure all three real buyers will see it.

5-Day.com

I've set up a 5-Day Web site on the Internet, 5-Day.com. If you visit the site, you'll see I've posted information in answer to the most frequently asked qestions about the 5-Day process.

I've also provided space for people running 5-Day sales to list information. Please note, I've done this merely as a courtesy. As I've already mentioned, the Internet is not a good place to advertise a 5-Day sale.

While it can't hurt to advertise on the Internet, it probably won't help much either. Again, place your ad where you can be sure all three real buyers will see it.

What Your Ad Should Say

You'll need a total of seven lines, eight at most. Don't waste space on phrases like "a real charmer" or "too cute to be true." If buyers come to your home and call it a real charmer, fine, but most people aren't looking for charm or cuteness—they're looking for homes.

Work hard on the part where you describe your home. Mention only the most important features.

Your ad should include these essential elements:

1. The location of the home
2. The fact that you're selling it yourself
3. A brief description
4. A low starting price
5. You'll take the best reasonable offer
6. You'll sell your home on Sunday night to the highest bidder
7. Your area code and telephone number

Remember, the sole purpose of the ad is to get calls. When you have potential buyers on the phone, you can give them as much detail as they want to hear.

What It Should Look Like

Your ad should look like this:

```
78 ST. E.                              BY OWNER
Studio  Bath  Kitchen  Elev.  Maint $595
Doorman   Beautiful Lobby in Elegant Bldg.
       $24,500 or Best Reasonable Offer
           Inspection Sat.–Sun. 10–5
          Co-op will be sold Sunday Night to
HIGHEST BIDDER              (608) 555-3138
```

It will work in almost any newspaper format.

The formula is simple:

The location of your home goes in the upper left-hand corner, flush left, in uppercase (capital) letters. The words "BY OWNER," also in uppercase, go in the upper right-hand corner, flush right.

The next two lines describe your home. In most newspapers you can get about 35 characters on each line. If your newspaper allows more characters per line, there's no problem. If your newspaper allows fewer characters per line, you must work out your layout before placing the ad. You may need extra lines to convey all the information.

The price and the words "or Best Reasonable Offer" should be centered on the fourth line. (Make sure the words "Best Reasonable Offer" are spelled out. Don't use the abbreviation BRO or B/O.)

"Inspection Sat.–Sun. 10–5" goes on the fifth line, centered.

"House will be sold Sunday Night to" goes on the sixth line, centered.

"HIGHEST BIDDER" appears in the lower left-hand corner, flush left, uppercase.

Your telephone number, including area code, is in the lower right-hand corner, flush right. (Numbers appear in uppercase format.)

Your ad should be all uppercase on the top and bottom lines—flush left and flush right. The lines in between should be centered, upper- and lowercase. This format gives your ad a very finished appearance. The white space in the ad makes it noticeable on a page full of ads with little white space.

It's not a tragedy if you add a line to your listing because your home is so feature-laden that two lines of description are not sufficient. But the description of your home is not what will sell it.

The starting price in your ad is the single most important feature. Be sure it's low enough to attract 25 calls by Friday night.

How to Place It

Prepare yourself before you attempt to place your ad. This will not be as easy as you might think. Ad takers may try to hurry you. Don't let them. This ad is very important to you. You will spend a substantial amount of money on it. Take the time to make sure it's right.

The ad taker may try to sell you a time period other than Wednesday through Sunday. Don't take it. You'll just drive yourself crazy if you add unnecessary days, or remove a margin of safety if you subtract days.

Other ad takers will advise you not to place your ad on Wednesday and Thursday. They'll suggest five different days. They're wrong. You need Wednesday and Thursday. Don't let anyone talk you out of using them.

Once you've convinced the ad taker you wish to place your ad from Wednesday through Sunday you must make sure the ad looks right. If you're dealing with a newspaper or an ad taker who's familiar with 5-Day sales, this will be no problem. They will know exactly how to set this ad in their newspaper.

If you're dealing with someone who has never set a 5-Day ad before, you must be very explicit. You must use the exact layout words I used in the previous section: "flush left," "flush right," "centered," "uppercase," "lowercase," etc. These words are used by newspaper people. If you use these words when you place your ad, the ad taker will understand you.

After placing the ad have the ad taker read it back to you. The ad taker should repeat all the layout words you used.

Lastly, buy copies of the periodicals in which your ad appears. Make sure your ad is in the right place and that it says what you want it to say. Check that the telephone number is printed correctly.

Wt Yr Ad Shd Nt LL*

The ad below makes every mistake in the book—and some new ones. It looks small on the page. It's unintelligible. It uses the same abbreviation to mean different things. The phone number doesn't have an area code.

```
N AtN B/O 5BR 3B HoP Dk P'i0
DR D/w/fp LR $99,500 or B/O I-SS
10–5 WBS Sun THB 555-3138
```

An ad like this will save the seller a few dollars in advertising costs because it uses fewer lines, but it will attact fewer buyers and cause the home to sell for thousands of dollars less.

Don't try to cram everything you can think of into a tiny ad by using abbreviations no one will understand. Just because brokers' ads are full of code doesn't mean they're good ads. If anyone asks what you mean by an abbreviation, drop it or change it. You're better off with a few understandable words than a lot of gibberish.

Remember, you're writing the ad for people just like you.

*What Your Ad Should Not Look Like

THE

CALLS

Uh-Oh Time

On Tuesday, in the middle of the night before the sale is scheduled to begin, you'll suddenly awake in a cold sweat, sit bolt upright in your bed, and begin to murmur, "Oh my God, what have I done?"

Don't worry! This is perfectly normal. It happens to everyone. When it hits, just pick up this book and turn directly to this page to refresh your memory on the following points:

1. There's no risk to you in this process if you follow this book and the advice of your attorney.
2. You're not the first one to try the 5-Day Method. Thousands of people all over the country have successfully used it. If you follow the book, price your home properly, and offer it to enough people, you'll sell it at the highest possible price.
3. The worst thing that can happen is that you lose a couple of hundred dollars and five days of your time. If nobody calls, you don't sell your home. You may feel a bit foolish, but you're no worse off than you were before.

Go back to bed, lie down, and try to get some sleep. You'll need it so you can answer the avalanche of phone calls you'll start getting tomorrow.

Keep a Phone Log

If you've offered your home at an irresistibly low starting price, and you've run your ad in the right places, the telephone will start ringing off the hook first thing Wednesday morning and continue to ring, almost without pause, until long after you've sold your home.

It's important to write down every call. You'll need a telephone log to determine how many people have called by Friday night. If you don't get 25 calls by Friday night, you'll use the telephone log to reach everyone who's called you to tell them you've postponed the sale. Once the sale begins it's helpful to refer to the log to see which callers have actually come.

Telephone logs are easy to maintain. Simply ask all callers their name and phone number. Add any identifying information picked up during the conversation.

This may seem like a waste of time, but it isn't. You'll be grateful to have callers' names and phone numbers in case you have to let them know about a change in plans. If you have 40 buyers during the inspection, there will be times when two or three families are in your home at once. Things will go more smoothly if you've made notes of their phone calls and can recall a snippet of conversation with them. Sometimes bidders' telephone numbers are illegible on the bidding sheet. If you've kept a telephone log you can refer to it to find the number.

Review the log the night before the first day of the inspection. Discuss notes and impressions with other family members who may have made entries. You'll find it easier to greet potential buyers at the door if you can put them into context. Someone may say, "Oh, I spoke to your daughter, she was very helpful," and this will be your introduction. If your daughter put information in the log, you might be able to say, "Yes, she mentioned your son was sick. Is he feeling any better now?"

Keep the telephone log handy during the inspection and refer to it after your initial contact with each buyer. In many cases a quick reference will refresh your memory and give you an opening to begin a conversation.

See the Sample Materials section, page 237, for a sample telephone log.

Everyone Can Help

Place a telephone log near each phone, along with a copy of all your printed materials, so anyone who picks up can answer the questions and maintain the log.

Work with your family. Make sure everyone realizes any caller could turn out to be one of the three real buyers. Go over all the printed materials together. Stress the importance of the telephone log.

Review the procedure for speaking to callers. If your children habitually answer the phone with lines like "It's your quarter, start talking" or "Appleby's Bargain Basement," try to dissuade them from this until your sale is over.

At first, everyone will be nervous. They'll want to hear how you handle the calls before they try it themselves. After a half-dozen calls, everyone should become adept at conversing with potential buyers.

The phone will continue to ring on Saturday and Sunday, when you'll be busy with buyers who come for the inspection. Make sure your telephone is properly covered for the entire five-day period.

When no one can answer the phone, don't turn on the answering machine. It's better for callers to get no answer, in which case they'll almost certainly call back, than to get a machine that might scare them away.

Structuring the Call

Give your callers as much time and information as they want. Some will keep you on the phone for half an hour, while others will just want the directions and nothing more. The constant repetition of the same information may become tedious, but you can't know if a real buyer will be the first caller or the hundredth, so you must have a productive conversation with everyone.

How you answer the telephone is the first thing a potential buyer will learn about you. Do nothing to drive buyers away. A nice, neutral "Hello" is a good starting point. The buyer will then say something like "I'm calling about the house for sale." "Would you like the long version or the short version?" is a good reply.

Regardless of which version they request, start by reading the Quick Description. Make sure you don't sound like an answering machine. Explain that you're reading this part of the script to everyone who calls. After you've finished, pause, and ask if they want to hear more.

Some will. Some won't.

If they want more information and don't ask specific questions, read them the Detailed Description, stopping occasionally to ask if they want to hear more.

After reading from the script, try to engage callers in a more personal conversation. By the end of the call the potential buyer should feel less like a stranger to you, and you should have some idea of who will be coming to inspect your home.

Don't allow callers to talk you into an early inspection. If they say they're working on Saturday and Sunday, offer to stay late for them Saturday night. Early inspections make other people feel that someone has somehow gained an advantage.

The Rule of 25

If you get 25 calls by Friday night, your ad worked.

If you didn't get 25 calls by Friday night your ad didn't work.

Twenty-five calls means 25 different people saw your ad and responded to it. Don't expect 25 real buyers. There aren't 25 real buyers.

Don't think just because you live in a rural area you can't get 25 calls. Start low enough, advertise in the right places, and you'll get 25 calls by Friday night—no matter where you live.

Count every call you get. Count people who immediately tell you they're not interested. Count brokers. Count speculators. Count developers. Count everybody. That's the way the rule works.

The rule of 25 is nothing more than a rule of thumb to see if your ad is working. The quality of the calls is not important. If 25 people seek you out at a time when most people get no calls at all, you can be sure you've got the attention of all three real buyers. That's all you care about.

Twenty-five calls is the absolute minimum. Fifteen is not nearly good enough, 20 is not enough. At least 25 different callers by Friday night is the rule. Get them and you'll have no problem with your sale.

It's okay to get 50 calls or 100 calls by Friday night. This will mean more work for you, but it will not change the selling price. If you get fewer than 25 calls by Friday night, stop the sale!

FINAL
TOUCHES

Ready...

When you run a 5-Day sale your home must look great—for just two days!

When you open your home for inspection you must not allow buyers to become distracted by any little thing that might bother them. It's easy to predict what will bother buyers. They're the same things that bother you.

When they first approach your home, everything should look neat and trim. The lawn should be mowed, the flower beds well tended. Shrubbery and trees should be trimmed. The driveway should be clean. There should be no bicycles or junk lying around.

The entryway should be inviting, with the outside light in good repair. Address numbers should be clearly marked. The doorknob should shine, the bell should sing.

Upon entering your home, buyers should immediately feel its owners are people of impeccable taste and breeding (like themselves). Your home should be uncluttered, the windows washed, carpets and floors spotless. Get rid of any extension cords lying around. Neaten shelves and desktops. Clean out the closets. Hang new shower curtains in the bathrooms, put out new towels, and make sure the soap dish doesn't look like something a mad scientist used for his experiments.

Turn on lights to make your home bright. Flowers are a nice touch. If necessary, cart away extra furniture. Rent a truck for two days and put into it everything that detracts from your home. Park the truck at a friend's house during the inspection period.

Organize the attic and air out the basement.

These are all little things. None will cost a lot of money, and all should be done to show off your home to its best advantage. You can do all this because you have to make this extraordinary effort for only two days.

Set...

You know how people ask you certain questions about your home over and over again. "Where's the powder room?" "Which door leads to the playroom?" "How do you get to the basement?" "Is there an attic?" You'll save yourself a lot of time and trouble if you put up signs to answer questions you know people will ask.

Buyers coming to your home will have other questions as well. They'll want to know room sizes. They'll want to know if curtains, fixtures, and appliances are included. Put up signs to answer these questions also. You won't regret it.

When the sale begins, you may find you didn't cover all the questions. Some things that are clear when you live in a home are not clear to someone who is doing a quick inspection. If several buyers ask the same question, put up another sign to avoid the confusion.

You'll have plenty to do without answering the same predictable questions over and over. Putting up signs will save you a lot of time and trouble. Your signs will also keep you from wearing yourself out before the round-robin.

Go!

If you've planned, advertised, and set up your sale properly, the rest is just a matter of following through on decisions that were made carefully when there was ample time to consider them. Go over everything in your mind. Run down the checklist on pages 251–252. Get a firm grip on which features you want to point out to buyers when they visit.

Make sure your home is ready to accept an onslaught of visitors at the appointed hour. Be prepared for early arrivals, but don't let them in before 10:00 A.M. Review your telephone log. Check names and any notes you made during conversations.

Lay out all your sheets in separate piles, one topic to a pile, along with a copy of this book. The materials should be placed on a counter or table, face up, near the entrance to your home. Don't preassemble the packets.

Move all pets out of your home. Don't just put them in the backyard— yapping dogs and yowling cats will drive some buyers to distraction and others will be allergic to them.

Make everything easy for your buyers. Is the front door hard to get to? Open the door you normally use and steer buyers in that direction. Is it raining? Park your car(s) somewhere else so buyers can enter through the garage. Plan what you'll do if the weather is inclement or some other unexpected event takes place. Let buyers see these things are not problems in your home.

Look forward to tomorrow.

Get a good night's sleep.

THE SHOW

Pace Yourself

A 5-Day sale is both physically and emotionally draining. Don't underestimate it. It'll be a long weekend.

You'll be answering the phone Wednesday, Thursday, and Friday while you're still taking care of the final details. Enlist the help of enough family or friends so you don't have to do everything yourself. You'll have some idea of how busy you'll be by the number of phone calls you get.

On Saturday you'll host one of the largest gatherings you've ever organized. Then you'll do it again on Sunday! Sunday night you'll conduct a major business transaction.

You'll meet a lot of people, many of whom you'll genuinely like. You'll both hear and tell a lot of stories. You'll have to concentrate on a lot of conversations.

In addition to the physical aspects, 5-Day sales are quite emotional. You are really going to sell your home Sunday night. You are really going to move. Your life is about to change. You'll be watching the bidding sheets, hoping and praying.

Make no plans for Saturday night. Get as much rest as possible. Don't go out or try to entertain. The phone will keep ringing. You'll be tired whether you realize it or not. You'll better understand what's in store for Sunday.

Sunday will be a longer and more difficult day. Not only will you run another open house, but you'll have to organize and run the round-robin as well. You'll try to make some sense out of the bidding sheets, but this is just preliminary bidding, so there is no pattern to it at all. If you feel yourself getting tired, call in reinforcements and take a nap. Be careful not to talk yourself out. You don't want to have laryngitis Sunday night.

Sunday night is the most critical part of the sale. You'll have to make many important decisions in a short time. You must be sharp.

Open House Signs

Decorate your neighborhood, and any reasonable approach to your home, with Open House signs to reassure buyers who are following your instructions that they're heading in the right direction. These signs will also attract local people who aren't actively looking for a home and won't see your ad in the newspapers.

The signs should feature an enlarged version of your classified ad on top. Below that, centered, it should say "Open House." Below that, place an arrow pointing left, right, or up. See the example on page 247.

Print the open house signs on 8½ x 11" fluorescent green or orange paper. These very brightly colored papers are available in larger stationery stores. Insert the printed signs in plastic sheet protectors used for loose-leaf binder presentations. The sheet protectors will keep the paper flat, and protect the sign in case of rain.

Get some removable Handi-Tak or Fun-Tak and some thumbtacks with large plastic heads. You'll be able to affix your signs to virtually any surface with either the Handi-Tak or the thumbtacks. Be generous with the Handi-Tak. It dries out quickly outdoors so you need a lot to ensure your signs will stay up all weekend.

Most buyers try to see as many homes as possible in a single day. They'll miss some of the homes because they can't find them. Make sure yours isn't one of the homes that's missed. Make it easy to find. When I put up signs, I think of them as clues in a treasure hunt where my home is the treasure and I want everyone to win.

Don't put up the Open House signs until Friday night at the earliest, or potential buyers will arrive before you're ready. Check your signs throughout the two days of your inspection. Replace those that have blown away or been taken down. Double-check to be sure all signs are pointing the right way.

I can't emphasize strongly enough the importance of Open House signs. I've conducted sales where all of the top bidders came as a result of open house signs.

After your sale is complete, be sure to take down every sign you put up. Your neighbors will tolerate the signs for two days, but you have an obligation to retrieve every last one of them by Monday night at the latest. Also, if you don't take them down, buyers will continue to show up at your door, which gets to be quite a nuisance.

Greeters

Teach greeters to welcome every buyer who enters your home. If one greeter is busy, another should be ready to step in. Never allow buyers to feel awkward when they enter. They shouldn't worry that they're walking into the wrong house or disturbing you from something you'd rather be doing.

Usually buyers will ring the doorbell before they enter, but sometimes unrelated groups come in at the same time. As buyers enter, a greeter should welcome them and walk them to the materials table. Make sure everyone is part of the same group. If not, ask another greeter to assist so a greeter is talking to each buyer group individually.

Don't preassemble printed materials. Greeters should assemble printed materials into complete packets as they speak with buyers. This allows the greeter to begin a conversation and explain each sheet individually.

Explain the bidding process. Point out this book. Tell buyers why you're home is being sold this way. Ask them if they'd like to look around. Show them where you'll be if they have questions. Ask if they'd like you to accompany them.

Every buyer should wind up with an information packet. If you see buyers who don't have your materials in their hands, it probably means they weren't properly greeted at the door. Approach them. Ask if they have your materials. If not, walk them over to the table and go through the normal welcome process.

Each sheet of your printed materials should be a different color so you can know from a distance which sheet is being read. If you see buyers lingering on specific sheets, you can approach them and ask if they need help. This is another way to start a conversation and get to know a potential buyer.

Don't confuse your open house with some kind of party. Don't serve tea and crumpets, or anything else. Don't watch television while your inspection is under way. Do nothing to distract the buyers.

Always remember your primary goal is to sell your home. You didn't invite these strangers to discuss sports or politics. Stay focused. Within a few welcomes, each greeter will be comfortable with the process and be able to easily repeat it throughout the inspection, hitting all the highlights every time.

Meanies, Soreheads, and Weasels

Everybody worries about what to do with meanies, soreheads, and weasels who show up at an Open House.

While it's true you may encounter an occasional meanie, it's been my experience that this is the exception, not the rule. Human nature is better than you've been led to believe.

Most 5-Day sales are almost festive occasions. A good time is had by all. There are no adversarial relationships here. You are ready for your guests. Friends and family are there to help you. The rules are fair and consistently applied. You're well organized, everyone is made to feel welcome, no one has come to pick a fight.

By restricting your inspection to 14 hours spread over two days you limit the risk of meanies. Arrange your sale to ensure you are never left alone. Your home should be constantly overflowing with buyers in addition to your family and friends. The phone will ring constantly. New people will continually enter your home. There is little opportunity for mischief.

Because the sale is conducted so openly you greatly reduce the sorehead problem. No one gets sore. All understand what they must pay to get your home. People don't leave the bidding angry, they just leave the bidding and congratulate you on getting such a high price for your home. No one will begrudge you that.

Weasels have nowhere to go, and they know it. If the top bidder starts weaseling on the deal, immediately drop down to the second bidder. Everyone can see you have more buyers than you have homes. You conclude your sale very quickly. Even if you must run another 5-Day sale, that's far better and less costly than trying to deal with a weasel.

THE CLOSE

Select a Closer

The most important person in a 5-Day sale is the closer. This person should be one of the sellers, preferably the one who will conduct the round-robin.

The closer should be clearly visible to buyers as they enter and should speak with all buyers before they leave. The closer should be located near enough to the door to be able to keep track of everyone who enters or exits. There should be enough seats near the closer so buyers and their families can sit down to discuss the questions they will undoubtedly have. Greeters should point out the closer, asking buyers to say "good-bye" on their way out.

The closer must determine which buyers are interested in the home and which are not. This is easily accomplished. After buyers have inspected the home, the closer asks each of them if they understand the bidding procedure. Some will say they're not interested in the home and leave. Most will be interested enough to hear the explanation.

Explain the Bidding

After buyers have had a chance to inspect your home, the greeter who originally welcomed them should approach and introduce them to the closer. The bidding sheets, attached to a clipboard, should be in open view near the closer.

The closer should pick up the clipboard and read the bidding terms on the Initial Bidding Sheet to each buyer. Review how the bidding will be conducted, and make sure each buyer understands the round-robin will be conducted over the telephone, Sunday night, starting at 8:00 P.M.

The closer should show all bids to every potential buyer so everyone knows the current status. Invite interested buyers to leave bids. Remind them that you will conduct the round-robin starting with the highest bidder, and that there's an advantage to bidding first.

The more who bid, the merrier. If they don't know what to bid, tell them to just put down one penny. They can always change their bid or they can wait until the end of the first round of the round-robin to hear what others have bid. I've seen people who started with a penny bid jump to $406,000—and buy the home.

The closer should explain to everyone that they're not bidding against you. They're bidding against all the other buyers they see. You're just the referee. You'll make sure everything is done fairly. You'll make sure everyone follows the rules you've laid out. You'll make sure the high bidder gets your home.

Many buyers will feel they don't have a chance and will be reluctant to bid. They will say they don't "win" anything. Encourage them to try. Remind them it costs nothing. They're under no legal obligation and they can always change their minds or change their bids.

The closer should try to spend time with each potential buyer. This will make everyone more comfortable during the round-robin bidding. You've gone to a lot of trouble to get these buyers to see your home. Don't let them off the hook now. Talk to every potential buyer. It's a lot of work, but it pays off.

The Tic-Tac-Toe Analogy

Everyone over the age of nine understands that whoever goes first in the game of Tic-Tac-Toe can't be beaten. If they know how to play the game, the worst they can do is tie.

The same is true in round-robin bidding. The first bidder has an enormous advantage.

The trick in round-robin bidding is to be the first to arrive at the price you think the home is worth, without paying more than you have to. The strategy for accomplishing this is explained in "How to Bid"(see pages 153–154).

Explain this to all buyers. Use the Tic-Tac-Toe analogy. Show them the "How to Bid" section in this book.

Real buyers are more inclined to leave higher bids if they understand it benefits them. Sometimes this results in a flurry of phone calls between 7:30 and 8:00 on Sunday night as bidders vie for the top position. If this happens it simplifies and shortens the round-robin, but does not change the final price.

Don't Tap Dance

Buyers will ask over and over if you will really take the high bid on your bidding sheets. Don't tap dance around this question. Know what your answer is and stick to it.

Here is your answer:

"If that's the best offer we get as of Sunday night, we'll take it!"

What's more, you *must* understand that's the true answer!

If 100 people go through your home and no one offers more than the amount in the newspaper, then your home isn't worth more than the amount in the newspaper!

You can count on people to behave in their own best interests. No one will let someone else walk away with a bargain. Each buyer wants to be the owner at the lowest possible price. If you start at a ridiculously low price, then that price plus $500 is still ridiculously low, and someone will bid it up.

This process will continue until the price gets to the reasonable range. Then the bargain hunters start dropping out, leaving the real buyers to bid up the price against each other.

You should see more than 100 strangers during your two-day inspection period. The time frame is too short for all those strangers to organize a conspiracy against you. They won't do it. They won't even think of it, because it's impossible.

When you tell people you'll take the highest bid you get, that's true! You must understand it's true, and you must say it in such a way that they believe you.

FOR THE BUYERS

What's Going On Here?

For most buyers this is likely to be the first 5-Day sale they've ever seen. They'll want to know why you're selling your home this way. Explain it to them with the help of this section.

There is nothing hidden about this process. Everything is done out in the open. It's surprising to most people, and most people love it. It's the way we always thought life was supposed to be.

Leave a copy of this book on a table where everyone can see it. Tell buyers you're using the 5-Day Method because you think it will result in the best deal for both you and them. Show them this chapter. Invite them to look through the book.

Make sure they understand there's no broker involved so you can afford to take a lower price for your home and still wind up with more money in your pocket. Make sure buyers understand they are not bidding against you, and that they are under no legal obligation as a result of the bidding process. They can back out if they change their minds.

Explain that they will have plenty of time to consult their settlement agent, review the terms of the sale, inspect the home, and obtain a mortgage in the conventional way. Make sure they understand the process is the same as conventional home sales once the round-robin is concluded.

You'll be surprised how many buyers ask you to help them bid. Show them this section.

How to Bid

1. Decide what you think this home is worth.
2. Decide what you are willing to pay for it. (This could be the same, more, or less than you think it's worth, but it should never be a round number.)
3. Figure out how to be the first to bid what you think this home is worth without offering more than you have to pay.

Example: Let's say you've responded to an ad for a home selling for $99,500 or best reasonable offer. You've looked at enough homes to know this is as nice as others that have just come on the market for $125,000. This home is as appealing as those that have been on the market for six months with a price dropped to $115,000.

You know any price under $110,000 is a steal, and that a price between $110,000 and $115,000 is a good deal. You figure the seller will get many bids under $99,500, but you can see that there are too many buyers for that to be the high bid. This home will probably sell for somewhere between $99,500 and $115,000. It could sell for more if someone really wants this particular home.

You are the first family to inspect the home. You are ready to buy. You want this home if you can get it at a good price. What should you bid?

Your initial bid should be $105,500.

A bid over the starting price tells the seller you are a serious buyer.

Your bid announces to other buyers that no one is going to "steal" this home from you. It scares off the professionals and simplifies the final bidding. Anyone else who wants this home is going to have to fight you for it.

You should call the seller before the inspection process is over to find out what the highest bid is. If the high bid on the "Initial Bidding Sheet" is greater than yours but less than what you are prepared to pay for the home, you should raise your bid so you will be the first one called in the round-robin. You already know any bid under $115,00 is a good deal for this home. If you jump to a higher level early, you will save yourself a lot of money later.

Do not stop at $115,000. Your top bid should be slightly above $115,000, perhaps as high as $117,500. When the bidding approaches $115,000 you should jump over it to your maximum.

Never announce to the seller that you are approaching your maximum. When you're done, just stop.

Testing Thresholds

Why did I suggest a "funny" number for the initial bid? Why not $105,000?

Buyers establish arbitrary threshold prices above which they tell themselves they will not bid. Most buyers use round numbers for thresholds. For this home, thresholds would come every $5,000: $100,000; $105,000; $110,000; and so on.

You should always take a position at least $500 above a threshold.

Spending $500 above an arbitrary threshold is not significant on a purchase price in excess of $100,000 that you will finance over a thirty-year period. By positioning yourself $500 over a threshold, you force the next bidder to consider a price $1,000 over the threshold. The third bidder will have to consider a price $1,500 over the threshold, and so on. By the time the bidding returns to you, it will be approaching the next threshold. If you still want the home, you would be wise to jump at least $500 over the next threshold.

If you're serious about buying the home, you must convince other bidders that you will always bid over their thresholds. You want to discourage all other bidders. You will pay less for the home if you test other buyers than if you allow them to test you.

The strategy behind bidding is to always have the strongest bidding position. Then, even if someone else makes a higher bid, you wind up exactly where you want to be. You have the right bid in your own mind. If the home sells for the price you are willing to pay, you will own it.

Preemptive Bidding

I feel I've tried to explain preemptive bidding a thousand times, almost always without success. Before the bidding, buyers think I'm just trying to drive up the price. After the bidding they approach me to say, "Now I get it—I would have saved a bundle if I'd made a preemptive bid."

If you really want a certain home and you know the current high bid is far under market value, you should make a bid that jumps two or more thresholds above the last bid. You know the home will never sell for anything like the current price. You want to discourage other potential buyers from thinking they just might wind up with this home.

Preemptive bids tell all other bidders that you intend to buy this home, no matter what it costs, and they will not be able to outbid you. That may not be true, but it is the message conveyed. Preemptive bidding is designed to make other buyers drop out before they hit their limits, which is exactly what you want them to do.

Probably the most interesting and effective preemptive bid is the one made by the first bidder in the round-robin. If the high bidder is just $500 above the pack, it makes sense to raise the bid. Surely someone else will bid another $500. The high bidder is wise to increase the gap in the bidding. This is the advantage of going first. The high bidder can put the bidding out of range of most, if not all, other bidders.

Failure to make a preemptive bid can expose you to the possibility of being pecked to death by ducks. I once witnessed a round-robin that went for 75 rounds and wasn't over until Wednesday night. During that time the price increased by $600,000. The two final bidders employed the same strategy. No matter what one bid, the other bid $500 more. Neither made preemptive bids. The home went for much more than it was worth. No one would drop out for $500.

Preemptive bidding is one of the best bidding strategies for buyers. Used early it will reduce the final selling price.

False Bids

I know you're wondering how you can be sure the seller won't put in false bids.

You can't know if the seller is putting in false bids!

It doesn't really matter.

This home will either sell for a fair price or it won't sell at all.

Review your bidding strategy. Know what this home is worth to you. Pay what you think it's worth, and no more.

The sellers have done the same thing. There is a price below which they won't be able to sell. They may make false bids until the bidding crosses that threshold.

Don't tell the seller when you're getting close to your limit. When you hit your limit, just stop. Without warning. This is the most effective way to bid. Other buyers will do the same thing. When it starts happening the seller will either stop making false bids or will wind up still owning the home.

Buyers know what homes are worth, and they won't spend more than they have to. Sellers don't know what their homes are worth. I have warned sellers throughout this book not to try to artificially raise the price. Even if they fool you today, you will realize your mistake before the settlement and you'll back out of the deal.

Cheating doesn't pay. False bidding doesn't work. As soon as the price goes over what you think the home is worth, stop bidding. The other real buyers will do the same thing. A 5-Day sale results in prices that are fair to both the buyer and the seller.

SELLING METHODS

Fixed vs. Negotiated Prices

In the United States, we buy most things on a fixed-price basis. When you walk into the supermarket there's a price on every item. You have just two choices. You can pay the price marked on the box or you can walk away. There's no middle ground.

Negotiated prices are another thing entirely. Many different systems are used.

The most common negotiated price mechanism generally goes by the name "haggling." In many countries haggling is the principal pricing technique. The buyer asks the price of an item for sale. The seller quotes a high price. The buyer says the price is ridiculous. Ritualized insults may follow as the seller and buyer work toward a price satisfactory to both.

In the United States, cars are often sold using the haggling technique. Most Americans say they don't like to haggle, but when things normally sold on a negotiated basis are offered at a fixed price, Americans, like everyone else, assume that's the starting price and begin to haggle.

Auctions are another technique used to negotiate prices. There are many different styles of auctions. Auctions are used to sell everything from antiques to tobacco.

Sealed bidding, open bidding, and round-robin bidding are other methods used to negotiate prices.

Homes are almost always sold for a negotiated price rather than a fixed price. Homes aren't like cereal boxes. They're not all the same. Even identical homes built in the same place at the same time aren't the same. Some have better views. Some have better neighbors. Buyers see the differences. They're willing to pay more for one home than for another. Prices must be negotiated.

Following are some of the techniques sometimes employed in the negotiated sale of homes.

Outcry Auctions

Outcry auctions are the kind run by antiques dealers and tobacco farmers where participants get together in a room and shout out their bids.

This type of auction is characterized by inadequate inspection times, incomprehensible rules, mind-numbing speed, and cash on the barrelhead. Ordinary people rarely buy anything of value at outcry auctions because they can't keep up with what's going on.

Outcry auctions are professional sales run by licensed professionals for professional buyers. You have neither the license nor the skill to be an outcry auctioneer. End-buyers are uncomfortable with outcry auctions, often failing to bid even if they think an item is worth the price.

Real estate developers who get into trouble will sometimes resort to outcry auctions to unload quickly as many properties as they can. These developers hire professional auctioneers, who receive sizable fees. Many properties are offered in a single day, one right after the next. Most properties have unstated minimum prices below which they will not be sold.

This is not what you're doing. You are not using the 5-Day Method because you're in trouble. You're using the 5-Day Method because it's the best way to sell your home. You're offering your home in a free market. You take bids at a leisurely pace. Potential buyers have enough time to carefully consider what they're doing. You have enough time to consider their bids.

You talk to each bidder individually, and make sure each understands exactly what is going on. There is no "bidding frenzy." You both come to an agreement as a result of the free market process, but neither party is legally obligated.

Be sure you understand you're not running an outcry auction. Be sure your buyers also understand the distinction.

Slow Dutch Auctions

Another type of professional auction is called the Dutch auction, where the auctioneer starts the bidding at a ridiculously high price no one will pay. The price is dropped until someone bites. These auctions are normally over in a matter of minutes.

Real estate brokers conduct "Slow Dutch" auctions. They put homes on the market at prices they know no one will pay. If the home doesn't sell in three months, the offering price is lowered. Three months later the offering price is lowered again. The price keeps dropping until a buyer is found or the seller is unwilling to drop the price further.

The Slow Dutch auction is the reason it takes so long to sell homes the conventional way. Everyone knows it's not smart to buy a home that has just been placed on the market. If buyers wait, the price will come down. Many buyers won't even look at a home until it's been on the market long enough for the price to have dropped several times.

The conventional pricing method, with a high price that slowly drops down to market level over time, is not good for the seller. It puts the seller under inordinate pressure for a protracted period of time. It will net the seller less money than the 5-Day Method.

Avoid the Slow Dutch auction.

Open vs. Sealed Bidding

The 5-Day sale features a bidding method called "open bidding." In open bidding, all bids are disclosed to all buyers at all times. The bidding unfolds where everyone can see it, over a two-day period. Open bidding favors nonprofessional buyers. People who don't know the exact fair market price are more likely to leave bids when the bidding is open.

Professionals will try to talk you into sealed bidding, where they have the advantage. In sealed bidding, each prospective buyer submits a bid sealed in an envelope. All the envelopes are opened at the end of the sale, and the highest bidder gets the home. Professionals know what they can afford to pay, and they know sealed bidding will scare off end-buyers. This will allow them to buy your home for less.

Another reason to avoid sealed bidding is that bids may be tens of thousands of dollars apart. One of the great advantages of round-robin bidding is you wind up with two or three top bidders within a thousand dollars of each other. If the top bidder balks for any reason, you simply drop down to the next bidder.

In sealed bidding you generally don't have that luxury. If the top bidder becomes difficult you must decide whether to renegotiate the price or run the sale all over again. The top bidder has the upper hand. Bidders know the spread between their bid and the next bid. They're in a position to force the issue. You'll either accept their terms or lose the sale.

Sealed bidding also runs a larger risk of collusion. For all you know, the second or third or fourth bidder is working in collusion with the top bidder. Remember, you don't really know any of these people, and situations will develop if you allow them to. Don't let anyone talk you into sealed bidding.

How to Run a Round-Robin

The negotiated pricing technique used in 5-Day sales is called "round-robin bidding." It requires no professional expertise, is very fair to both the buyer and the seller, and usually results in a price satisfactory to both.

Leave time for yourself between the end of the inspection and the beginning of the round-robin. The last potential buyer may leave late. You may want to have a quiet dinner with your family. Start setting up the Round-Robin Bidding Sheets (see the Sample Materials section, pages 241–245) an hour before you plan to begin it.

Write down both the first and last names of the bidders, their phone numbers, and the amount of their bids. If a couple has bid together, try to get the names of both individuals even if they say only one of them will be doing all the bidding. Transfer all notes to the round-robin sheets, consulting your telephone log to confirm telephone numbers. Once the round-robin gets under way you should work only with the sheets you have just prepared.

Review names and histories with greeters. Try to know who everyone is before you start phoning. This will not be 100% possible. You won't remember everyone. But with the aid of notes and friends, you should be able to remember most people.

Start the bidding exactly when you told the bidders you would start. A good time is 8:00 P.M. It gives you enough time to unwind and set up. It gives buyers enough time to get home and have dinner. The typical round-robin runs for around 1½ hours, so if you start at 8:00 you'll be done by 9:30, which most people would consider a reasonable hour.

Re-read the terms at the top of the Round-Robin Bidding Sheet to each bidder so you can be sure everyone understands what is happening. Try to paint a picture for each as though he or she were standing beside you, watching the bidding. Tell them how many others are bidding. Tell them when other bidders drop out. Be fair and honest with all bidders, and they will be fair and honest with you.

Anticipate it will take an average of five minutes per bidder in the first round to establish contact, get the right party on the phone, review the terms, and determine if they are still interested. If you have twenty bidders, it will take about an hour to complete the first round.

When the first bidder has settled on a bid, call the second bidder. Continue this process until you've contacted all the bidders. Some will drop out immediately. Others will want to work with you on the phone. Tell each approximately when you expect to be able to call back. Don't allow a bidder to come back into the bidding after dropping out.

Once every bidder has been given a chance to bid, call the first bidder again. If no one has made a higher bid, the first bidder can buy your home at the bid price. If there has been a higher intervening bid, give every remaining bidder the opportunity to top that bid. Subsequent rounds go more quickly, and you'll get to know the real buyers better.

Continue this process until a high bid emerges and no other bidder wishes to top it. Never rush the bidding. This is a major purchase. The actual bidding can create unexpected situations, so give each buyer enough time. Sometimes buyers need to consult a spouse, a parent, or a business partner. If it takes too long, call the other bidders and explain what's happening. Use your best judgment. Wait as long as you can. Then move on, or tell the bidder to get back to you within a certain time period.

Don't stop the bidding too soon. If people get tired, stop and resume Monday night if that is satisfactory to all remaining bidders. After everyone has dropped out except the high bidder, pause for five minutes. Give the second bidder enough time to reconsider the final bid. Many times the second bidder will call back to reenter the bidding. After a pause of at least five minutes, call the top bidder to tell them they've got the house

Don't Cheat!

You may feel a strong temptation to bid against your buyers. Resist it!

This method works perfectly without any help or intervention from you.

I've heard from sellers who entered the bidding and outbid all the real buyers because they thought or were told they could get more. Six months later they still owned their homes. Not only could they not get more, they couldn't even get what they had been offered!

They want to know what to do now!

There is only one thing to do: start all over again—and this time, play fair!

Honesty *is* the best policy.

"WHAT TO DO IF..."

You're Having a Problem

Your 5-Day sale should closely follow this book. If it does not, you're having a problem. Solve it immediately. Don't try to reinvent the wheel. This is no time to be creative.

If the market says your home is worth less than the lowest price you would possibly consider, then it is worth less than the lowest price you would possibly consider. You'll know if that's the case by Friday night. Face it, and decide what you're going to do.

This may mean you can't afford to sell your home. It may mean you'll have to take less than you want. In either case, stop the sale. Don't think things are going to get better if you just wait it out. That won't happen. You'll just get yourself into trouble. Run your ad another weekend at a lower starting price, or keep your home.

This section deals with the problems most common to 5-Day sales. These problems are both easy to spot and easy to fix.

No One Calls

Remember, 5-Day ads always work. If yours fails to attract 25 calls by Friday night, you've made a mistake. Maybe you picked the wrong newspapers. Maybe you forgot to include your telephone number. Maybe your ad isn't clear.

Most likely, your starting price is too high. You advertised the price you hoped to receive instead of the price buyers hoped to pay. Your starting price did not make it clear to potential buyers that your home will definitely be sold to the highest bidder Sunday night.

You should get around a half-dozen calls by Wednesday night. You should have a dozen calls by Thursday night. You *must* have at least 25 calls by Friday night. If you get fewer than 25 calls by Friday night, you've made a mistake.

Stop the sale, pull the ad, and tell anyone who calls subsequently that the sale has been postponed. Go back to your telephone log, call everyone on it, and tell them you've postponed the sale because you didn't get enough calls. Tell them you plan to run the sale again within a few weeks, starting at a lower price.

Ask them if they'd like you to call them when you decide to run your sale again. Of course they'll say "yes": they thought your original price looked good—now you're going to lower it!

In all likelihood some of the buyers who called are real. But you can't be sure all the real buyers will attend. Stop your sale! Any other course exposes you to risk.

No One Comes

In a typical 5-Day sale a small group of highly interested buyers will arrive early Saturday morning. More people will arrive Saturday afternoon. Sunday morning is generally slow because many people go to church, while others sleep late. Sunday afternoon is often the busiest time of all, as latecomers rush to beat the deadline and interested buyers return for a second look.

Inclement weather may alter this pattern but should not change the total number of buyers.

If you get 100 calls, and 50 to 75 people say they're interested, you can expect 25 to 40 families to attend your open house. Generally the first buyers will be there by 10:00 A.M. Saturday morning.

If no one has come by noon, Saturday, send someone out to check your signs and make sure the road to your home is clear.

If you see people pulling into your driveway but they never get out of the car, it means they feel you have substantially misrepresented either your home or your neighborhood, and they can tell from afar they don't want to live there.

Don't make this mistake. If buyers feel they can't trust you, they won't bid on your home. When they drive up, every buyer should feel your home is better than they thought it would be. Even if your home is located in the middle of a chemical dump, someone will buy it at the right price. Chemical companies have proved this all over the county.

If no one comes, run another 5-Day sale. Drastically drop the starting price. When buyers call, emphasize the problems. They'll come. They'll bid. They'll buy.

No One Bids

If no one bids, your closer is not doing the job properly. The closer should be able to coax a penny bid out of almost anyone. Most of these penny bids are worthless, but they will encourage real buyers to enter the bidding.

When asked if you would really take one penny for your home, you must keep repeating, "If that's the highest bid we get by Sunday night, we'll take it." Don't worry. Someone else will bid two cents. Someone will bid a dime. Finally, the real bidding will begin.

Don't be concerned if no bid on the initial bidding sheet is acceptable. This often happens. It just means your buyers don't want to reveal their bidding strategy. It will result in many more participants in the round-robin; the round-robin will take longer, but you'll get exactly the same final price.

Play fair. Don't insert your own bids. When the round-robin bidding begins, buyers will understand they control the bidding. They will know they are bidding against each other, and they are not bidding against you. Then they will start bidding seriously as they realize they could really wind up owning your home at a price they consider fair.

The High Bid Isn't High Enough

Check with your settlement agent on this!

The law varies from state to state. In some states nothing you agree to is final until a contract is signed. In other states, nothing is final until the settlement.

When I run a 5-Day sale I always take the top bid. I'm absolutely convinced the high bid you get in a properly run 5-Day sale is the highest bid anyone can get at this time.

If you owe the bank more than you get from the sale and you can't make up the difference, you'll have to negotiate with both the bank and the top bidder. Explain the situation to each. See what can be done. The sale won't close without the bank's approval. Sometimes the high bidder will pay more to get the house. Sometimes the bank will take less than they're owed to get rid of a problem. Sometimes someone figures out a middle ground where everyone gets what they want, and no one gets hurt.

The important thing to recognize is that the high bid you get is probably the highest bid anyone can get for your home at this time. That's what your home is worth today.

You Get Crazy Bids

During the inspection, somebody will poke you in the ribs and say, "Yeah, but what if I offered you a million dollars for this home, right on the spot? I'll bet you'd take it!"

Wrong.

If someone offers you much more than you know your home is worth, something is wrong with the deal. The check will be bad; the money counterfeit; the buyers will want to change the terms; the bank won't grant a mortgage. It will almost certainly fall through. You'll be left high and dry— and it will serve you right!

You wrote the rules for this sale. You play by your rules. There is no reason for anyone to offer you a million dollars for a home that's worth only $125,000. If it happens, it's a trick.

In all probability no one will offer you a million dollars for a $125,000 home, but someone could say, "I'll give you more than anyone has bid so far if you stop the bidding and let me have the home right now."

Don't do it.

Instead of three buyers you'll have just one. If something happens to that buyer, you'll have none. People who came to see your home only to be told you changed the rules are not likely to come back a second time. Keep in mind that the buyer pool has only a certain number of buyers and you may have to jump into the pool a second time.

You're Offered Crazy Deals

In a conventional real estate sale you rarely have a multitude of buyers at any one time. Your broker presents a buyer. The buyer offers a deal. You decide whether to accept or reject the deal that's offered.

The buyer may propose a crazy deal that concludes with your receiving two toads and a chicken as a down payment. That may be the best deal that you can get, and you may indeed decide to take it. If you reject the deal, there is no telling how long you'll have to wait for the next acceptable deal to come along.

But when you sell your home using the 5-Day Method, you'll be offered many different deals at the same time. You can pick and choose what is best for you. Some may offer more money in return for partial owner financing. Some may offer cash in return for a lower price. Most will opt for conventional bank mortgage financing.

You must know what you want. You must think about it and figure it out in advance. During the final five days you won't have the time to calculate. Be prepared.

From the 40 to 100 buyers who inspect your home, you can expect a dozen serious bids, six of which should approach what you consider fair.

If you have a preference for one type of buyer over others, or you're prepared to make financial concessions to get a faster closing, let this be known to all the buyers before the bidding begins. Some may have the ability to fit into your preferred category if they know this will make it easier for them to buy your home.

The Bidder Disappears

You will have difficulty establishing contact with some bidders when you begin your round-robin. Some will get stuck in traffic. Others will forget about the bidding. If you get no answer, double-check the telephone number. If it's right, move on to the next bidder. If you get an answering machine, leave a message.

If the missing bidder is also the top bidder, you must discard the top bid. Explain to all other bidders what happened and how you have dealt with it. Tell them that you will try to contact any missing bidders in the second round. Remind them all that you know none of them.

Once you've gone completely through the first round of the round-robin, again try every bidder you missed the first time around, including the answering machines. Some will now be home and will be anxious to join in the bidding. If you get a machine a second time, leave a second message. Then forget about it and move on.

Bidders who can't be reached during the round-robin are invariably bidders who don't want to be reached at all. They wanted to be big shots during your inspection. They bid more than they have. Now they've disappeared. Don't be angry with them. They advanced your bidding. They participated. They helped you.

If bidders really had an unexpected problem, they will call you during the round-robin to explain and ask to reenter the bidding. The round-robin generally lasts for more than an hour. That's plenty of time for anyone to find a phone and call in. If you believe their story, and they wish to honor their original bid or advance a higher bid, you may allow them to reenter the bidding.

This is a dangerous situation for you. You will have to interrupt the flow of the round-robin. Other bidders won't like what they hear. They may think you are trying to manipulate the bidding. Listen to what you're saying from their point of view. Does it sound hokey?

Don't allow bidders to enter the round-robin late unless you're absolutely convinced they are telling you the truth. This situation rarely occurs. Real buyers are where they're supposed to be when they're supposed to be there. If something happens, they generally get to you before you call them.

Real buyers will go out of their way. They want your home. Even if the round-robin falls at an inconvenient time, they'll make sure you have some way to reach them or they will select a surrogate to bid for them.

The Deal Falls Through

Things don't work out perfectly every time. Some deals fall through.

Impress on your settlement agent that speed is of the essence in your sale. If the deal falls through early, you've still got two or three buyers lined up to buy your home. If for any reason the top buyer drops out, you simply drop down to the next.

But if you can't rescue the deal, you'll simply have to run the 5-Day sale again. This is not as bad as it seems. Most of the work is done, and you know exactly what to expect. You can correct any mistakes you feel you may have made the first time around.

You can rerun the sale as soon as you're ready. Some people who attended the first time will call. They will ask you what happened. Tell them the truth. They don't have to come back to see your home again if they don't want to. They can simply enter the bidding over the phone. Many will.

All the rules remain the same. The rule of 25 remains in effect. You will get some different buyers, although many will be the same if you run the second sale very close in time to the first. You will be amazed at how close the final bid in the second sale is to the final bid in the first.

I know a guy in New York City whose co-op board kept turning down his high bidder. He sold the same apartment, using the 5-Day Method, three times—for the exact same price each time. I know a woman in New Jersey who sold her home twice using the 5-Day Method. Her starting price was $100,000 lower the second time than the first. She got the exact same amount of money each time.

You Must Reschedule the Sale

If you must reschedule a 5-Day sale, first look at the calendar. The best time for buyers would be on the following weekend. But if the problem will last for more than a week, or a holiday is coming up, or the next weekend is inconvenient, you may have to postpone the sale for more than a week.

Tell every caller why you've rescheduled and when the sale will be held. Then go through your regular drill, reading from your information sheets, entering the calls in your telephone log, and getting the callers' phone numbers in case there's another change of plan.

If you kept a good phone log, you can call all interested parties to advise them of the new date for the inspection and sale. If people you were unable to reach arrive to inspect your home, make them feel welcome to do so and explain why you've postponed the sale. Tell them you called everyone who left a phone number and that you're sorry you were unable to reach them.

Start all over again the Wednesday prior to the new sale date. You'll have to place your ad again. This is unfortunate, but it's much less costly than selling your home cheap. Run your sale as if nothing had happened.

You Change the Price

Sometimes people get so backed into a corner that they must sell on a certain weekend whether the 5-Day Method is working or not. Some are just days away from bankruptcy or a forced move. Others can't schedule another five-day period in the near future. When they don't get enough calls, they lower the price in their ads and they inform all the previous callers of the price change.

You can get away with this, but it increases your risk.

If you must proceed with your sale by lowering your price, be sure you lower it enough because there will be no turning back. Don't lower the price incrementally. Lower it drastically! You won't get another chance.

With a low enough starting price for *three* days you can still get 100 telephone calls and 40 to 50 buyers. You can still sell your home. But you cannot be sure to get the highest possible price. You cannot be sure all three real bidders will show up.

My experience with people who have drastically lowered their price by Friday is that most sell their homes. My guess is that in 85% of these cases the sellers got the same price they would have received if they had run the lower starting price for five days.

Sometimes you just have no choice. Sometimes you simply have to take a risk.

Your Home Is an Oddball

What about oddballs? What if you can't imagine anyone would want your home? Maybe it's in bad shape or it's located next to a nuclear power plant. What if it's so far off the beaten path you despair of anyone even finding it?

You bought your home. *You* overlooked some things and made allowances for others. For some reason your home was attractive to you. And at a certain price, it will be attractive to a lot of other people, too.

"Contemporary," or "modern," homes are a different kind of oddball. No matter what selling method you use, these homes are the most difficult to sell. Contemporary homes are one-of-a-kind, designed by architects to reflect the desires of the original owners. They generally defy description. Buyers only know what these homes are *not*. They're not colonial, they're not ranch, they're not Tudor, they're not Cape Cod. Buyers have no clear picture of what they *are*.

There are as many subcategories of contemporary homes as there are styles of homes: horizontal, vertical, symmetrical, asymmetrical, square, trapezoidal, round, etc. Some are in the earth, others are in trees. Some use traditional building materials, others use highly nontraditional building materials.

Contemporary homes were built to the taste of the original owner, generally at great expense. Interior layouts often reflect specific needs. It's far more difficult to locate a second owner with the same taste, needs, and money. Many buyers who are interested in contemporaries underestimate building costs and think they can build a home to their own specifications for less than the selling price of existing contemporaries.

Contemporaries purchased from original owners often sell for less than they cost to build. They tend to have a lower resale value compared to traditional homes of comparable square footage on similar land. There may not be three real buyers for a contemporary at any given time.

If you want to sell a contemporary using the 5-Day Method you will have to modify many rules in this book:

1. Your starting price should be half what you want to receive.
2. You must leave yourself a safety valve so you don't have to sell your home if the price is not high enough. (Consult your settlement agent on this.)
3. You must advertise more widely.
4. You probably won't get 25 calls by Friday night.
5. You may have to negotiate directly with your high bidder.
6. It may take longer than five days.

Selling contemporaries using the 5-Day Method is possible, but not easy. The regular rules don't apply.

For most other oddballs, the 5-Day Method works just as well as it does on more traditional homes. It doesn't matter how rural you are. The condition of your home doesn't matter. Your location doesn't matter. You can describe all those things in your ad and over the phone. People can get a clear picture of what you have for sale. At a certain price there will be plenty of buyers. All the regular rules apply.

TRANSFERRING OWNERSHIP

Your Government Can Help

You'll need professional help transferring ownership of your home.

To better understand this process, get a copy of a U.S. Department of Housing and Urban Development booklet entitled "Settlement Costs." It's free, and you can get one from any residential mortgage loan provider.

This thirty-page page booklet answers questions you don't even know to ask. It's well written, easy to understand, comprehensive, and up-to-date. It explains terms and concepts used when you're transferring ownership of a home—a process called "settlement."

Once you've gone through the booklet you'll better understand what's involved, who can help you, and how to negotiate the fees you'll have to pay.

Settlement Agents

Settlement techniques vary all over the country. In some places people use attorneys, in other places they use escrow companies, title insurance companies, and lending institutions. Practices vary within states and even within cities. You should line up your local settlement agent before your sale begins.

You can use your settlement agent for advice before the sale, but the agent's most critical role is to be ready to move on the Monday morning after the sale.

You want the time between the bidding and the settlement to be as short as possible. This is where your settlement agent comes in. Your agent will qualify the buyer, protect your interests, obtain all necessary documents, and certify that everything has been done legally.

Establish timetables with your settlement agent. If your agent fails to move on your sale in a timely manner, find another. Right away. If your agent senses your buyer is pulling back, make sure you know about it. Right away.

Immediately after you've negotiated your deal with the buyer, get the name and phone number of the buyer's settlement agent, and give this information to your agent along with all details about the conditions of the sale.

The two agents will then work everything out between themselves. They will contact the banks, arrange for title searches and title insurance, write up all contracts, calculate conveyance fees due to state and local governments, and come up with a simple piece of paper that explains how much you'll get when all is said and done.

You can rate settlement agents by how quickly and smoothly everything moves. If the process starts to bog down, and you know it's not your agent's fault, the problem has to be with either the buyer or the buyer's settlement agent. Seriously consider contacting the next bidder on your list if this happens.

Settlement agent fees vary and are negotiable. They generally run between $250 and $750, depending mainly on where you live. If your settlement is complicated, your fees may run higher. Try to keep the settlement as simple as possible by culling out complex deals at the time of the bidding.

Going to Contract

The contract sets up the settlement. You use the contract to ensure that the settlement will come as soon as possible after the sale. It's in your interest, both financially and psychologically, to settle your home quickly.

Among other things, the contract will stipulate:

- The amount of the sale
- The timing of the sale
- The timing of transfer of funds
- What is included in the sale
- What is excluded from the sale
- How the title will be conveyed
- How taxes, assessments, and fees for delivered fuel and miscellaneous items on the property will be apportioned
- Who is responsible for insurance
- The condition of the premises
- The location and timing of the settlement
- Obligations in case of a default
- Everything else that may in any way affect the sale

In most cases, your settlement agent will write the contract and send it to the agent for the buyer. The buyer's agent will review the contract with the buyer to verify that everything in it agrees with the buyer's understanding of the deal. They may ask for changes or modifications.

When you and the buyer and both settlement agents agree to the contract, you and the buyer will sign it. Its provisions then go into effect, and the remainder of the sale is conducted in accordance with what's in the contract.

Sometimes the contract requires a down payment to be made immediately. This down payment may range from $1,000 to around 10% of the purchase price and is kept in escrow by your settlement agent. The down payment (often called "earnest money") is one way for you to determine quickly whether or not the buyer intends to go through with the sale.

Usually the down payment is not refundable if the buyer fails to live up to obligations set forth in the contract. These obligations are to seek a mortgage within a certain amount of time, to inspect the property on a timely basis, and to be prepared to settle on the house by a certain date. If the buyer is unable to get a mortgage, or discovers that you've materially misrepresented your home in any way, the deal is off and the down payment *is* refunded.

Your settlement agent's job is to write the contract and get the down payment as quickly as possible. An experienced settlement agent will have been through this process hundreds of times and will know if requests made by the buyer are customary.

"Putting it on paper" is a very important safety check for both you and the buyer. It forces the buyer to come up with some of the money. It lets you know immediately whether or not the buyer is serious. It establishes a timetable for the sale. It confirms that everyone understands and agrees to the deal.

The Settlement

The settlement is the actual transfer of ownership from you to the buyer. Cash settlements are generally quicker and less complicated than settlements where financing is involved. In a cash settlement, there is no mortgage.

After the settlement you no longer own your home, and someone else does.

In closing settlements there is a final meeting between you, your settlement agent, and the buyer and buyer's settlement agent; this is when you get the money and the buyer gets the home. Dozens of pieces of paper are signed on the spot, all of which your settlement agent will explain to you during the closing, prior to your signing.

Other people may be there, representing title insurance companies, banks, and any other parties with an interest in what is going on. If both you and your spouse are selling the home, then both of you should be there. The same is true for the buyer if more than one individual is involved.

A closing may be held in a settlement agent's office, in a room made available by a bank, in a title insurance company room, or anywhere else that has a large table with enough chairs, a degree of privacy, and a nearby photocopy machine.

The buyer's settlement agent or bank will give your agent a certified check. Your agent will write a check to your bank to pay off your mortgage, as well as checks to cover all city and state taxes Your agent will receive a check from you to cover settlement fees, or will deduct the fee from the check you finally receive after everyone else has been paid.

Within an hour or an hour and a half, you should have in your hand one of the biggest checks you've ever seen, and the buyer should own your home.

In escrow settlements the same things happen, but none of it is done face to face. All parties to the deal give checks, contracts, insurance, etc., to settlement agents, who put it in escrow. When everything is in place, the settlement agents file paperwork, retain fees, and send out checks to complete the transaction.

It's not over until you have the check in your hand! Sometimes homes fail to settle for the weirdest reasons. Sometimes the buyer simply doesn't have the money (and never tells anyone). Sometimes there's a snag in the title search or title insurance. Sometimes someone gets cold feet and the whole deal falls through. Sometimes these things happen at the very last possible moment.

You can fail to settle even when the most diligent settlement agents are involved. Try to structure the settlement in such a way that if it falls through, for any reason, you're not financially ruined.

APPENDIX

Open-Book Math Quiz

(There are no trick questions in this section.)

If you understand the answers to this quiz, then you'll understand why you should use the 5-Day Method. I know you want to skip this part but please resist that temptation. I'll provide the answers. When you're done, you'll understand things I can't explain any other way. You'll make a lot of extra money if you understand the math.

Grade yourself. Calculators allowed.

Let's start with a simple problem.

1. Which home sale will put more money in your pocket?
   - A. $100,000 selling price minus $6,000 commission.
   - B. $95,000 selling price—no commission.

   The answer is B. $95,000 is more than $94,000. That was easy. (They're all easy.)

2. Which home sale will put more money in your pocket?
   - A. Sell home in five days for $100,000.
   - B. Wait six months, sell for $105,000—pay $10,000 taxes and interest.

The answer is A. $100,000 is more than $95,000.

3. Which home sale will put more money in your pocket?
   A. Sell home for $98,000 cash. Settle the following week.
   B. Sell home for $100,000. Settle two months later. Pay $2,000 taxes and interest.
   C. You'll put the same amount in your pocket either way.

   The answer is C, but A is the better deal because there's less time for things to go wrong.

See, that wasn't so hard. The point of the math quiz is that you must not be blinded by selling prices. People will always ask you "What did the house sell for?" This question misses the point. The right question is "How much money did you put in your pocket?"

Pricing Worksheet

Are You Ready to Sell Your Home?

1. What is the most you would pay for your home? $_____

2. What is the least you would take for your home? $_____

3. If line 2 is greater than line 1, you will have trouble selling your home. $_____

Determine the Ballpark Price

4. Multiply line 2 times .9 $_____

Confirm Your Ballpark Price

5. Look for other homes like yours. Your ballpark price must be at least 10% below any other listed price for a similar home. If it is not, lower it. Your confirmed ballpark price is $_____

Find a Magic Number

6. Subtract $25,000 from line 5. $_____

7. Subtract another $25,000 if line 5 is greater than $250,000. $_____

8. Magic numbers always end with 24,500; 49,500; 74,500; or 99,500. If the number in line 7 ends in any other number, drop down to the next lowest magic number. $_____

Make Sure Your Price Is Irresistible

9. Ask friends and family if they would buy your home for your magic number. They should tell you you're crazy. Your magic number should be so low anyone would jump at it without hesitation. If they don't, keep lowering from magic number to magic number until everyone agrees your price is irresistible. Your irresistible price is $_____

Test the Market

10. If you're convinced the price on line 9 will attract 25 buyers by Friday night, use it as the starting price in your ad.

Q & A

Q. If a two-day open house is good, is a four-day open house better?

A. No! Do NOT extend your inspection. The process works in part because of the excitement of the event. Don't stretch it out!

Your open house should last for two days—let the excitement build—don't reduce the number of people in your home by allowing them to come over a greater period of time.

Q. My home is worth much more than $100,000. Shouldn't the bids be farther apart than $500?

A. Absolutely Not! No one gives up a home for a difference of $500. In small jumps, buyers will go thousands of dollars over their preset limits. Remember that $500 jumps mean people must bid at least $1,000 more than their last bid. (The other bidder topped them by $500, now they must go up another $500.)

You don't care how many phone calls you have to make. Think of it as dialing for dollars. If you could make $500 for a 20-second phone call, and do it over and over again, wouldn't you want to do it as many times as you can?

Larger jumps will stop the bidding sooner. That is exactly what you don't want. Separate the bids by $500 no matter what your home is worth.

Q. What do you think of trying a "test run" the weekend before the actual sale?

A. Don't do it! It confuses the buyers, costs more money, and accomplishes nothing.

Wednesday through Friday is your test run. Your goal is 25 calls. If you get 25 calls by Friday night it means your test worked and you can safely continue with your sale. *If you fail to get 25 calls by Friday night you must stop the sale.* This is the only test run you need.

Q. Shouldn't I ask bidders for a deposit when they make their bids?

A. No. Do nothing to discourage bids. You want everyone to bid. You don't really care whether or not they have the money at this point. You want them to advance the bid. Most of the people who bid will not be the final buyers. Only one will. Deal only with that person after the bidding is over. Move the high bidder to a contract as quickly as possible.

Q. Are some homes too rural for the 5-Day Method?

A. You can't be too rural! I've worked with people in the bayous of Louisiana who lived ten miles outside some town a hundred miles from any town you've ever heard of. After trying to find a buyer for more than two years, their broker told them their home was too rural. So they tried the 5-Day Method. One hundred people called. Forty people visited their home. They sold that home in five days, and got more than they were hoping for.

I can tell you virtually the same story about people in Maine; in Alaska; in Hawaii; in Montana. If your starting price is low enough, you will attract all the real buyers and they will bid against each other. The 5-Day

Method works no matter where you live.

Q. Shouldn't I base my starting price on "comps"?

A. No. "Comps"—broker jargon for prices asked or paid for similar homes—mean nothing. Your home is somehow different from every other home. You are selling it at a different time. The buyer pool is different. However slight these differences may seem to you, they add up in the minds of buyers. This may make your home sell for substantially more or substantially less than other so-called comparable homes.

People who compile lists of comps are trying to make a point. They pick and choose what is comparable to prove the point they are trying to make. They will fail to include home sales that refute their point. For example, I recently spoke to a woman who wanted to base the price of her condo on the price just received by the woman across the hall. She neglected to mention the woman across the hall had a sea view, while she had a trash-dump view.

When you use the 5-Day Method you are not trying to guess what your home is worth. You must start with a price substantially below any other comparable home on the market. You can't start too low. Use my pricing worksheet on pages 217–218. Forget about comps.

Q. What is a "reserve"?

A. In Outcry Auctions, a reserve is an amount below which an item won't be sold. This "reserve" may be stated or hidden. The seller has given the auctioneer instructions to refuse to sell the item unless it goes for more than a certain amount. In "unreserved" auctions, the sellers simply outbid the buyers so they won't have to deal with this issue. (The auctioneers don't care. They still get their fee.)

Q. Should I show bidders recent appraisals of my home?

A. No. Appraisals mean nothing and only serve to confuse buyers. I recently had two appraisals done on my home for mortgage purposes. They came in $250,000 apart. Clearly, either one or both of those appraisers was way off the mark.

Sellers don't show buyers appraisals lower than the current high bid. They only pull out higher appraisals in the hope this will spur buyers to bid more. But buyers often think the appraisals represent the lowest amount the seller will actually take, so they don't bid at all.

Buyers know what your home is worth to them. That's all that counts. Don't confuse them with appraisals.

Q. Should I push the top bidder if the house doesn't settle quickly?

A. Never. Establish a close working relationship with the top bidder. Play "Good Cop/Bad Cop," where you are always the good cop and the settlement agent is the bad cop. If some pushing must be done, let your settlement agent do it. Then, if there has been a misunderstanding, your buyer can still come back to you to straighten it out.

The only one you should ever push is your settlement agent.

Q. Am I obligated to sell my home even if the highest price isn't high enough?

A. Probably not. I'm not an attorney, so I can't give you legal advice. Each state writes its own real estate laws. The answer to this question varies from state to state. You *must* consult a real estate attorney on this one.

Don't just talk to your friend who happens to be a lawyer. Real estate law is highly specialized. Talk to a pro. I know dozens of real estate attorneys who've used the 5-Day Method. I've talked to real estate attorneys in many states who have advised me, without exception, that in their states you don't have to sell to the high bidder if the bid is not high enough.

Still, you must check with a real estate attorney in your state to be sure of the right answer for your situation.

Q. What's the hardest part of a 5-Day sale?

A. The hardest part of a 5-Day sale is being honest with yourself. Most people overvalue their homes. Then they hope they'll get more than they're hoping for. They never consider their home may be worth less than they're hoping for.

The beauty of the 5-Day Method is that, if run properly, it will consistently find the top end of the fair market value in exactly five days. You may not like what you learn, but the method doesn't lie.

Q. If the top bidder wants to change the terms should I renegotiate?

A. No. Never renegotiate. Settle as agreed or offer your home to the next bidder. This is one of the strengths of the 5-Day Method. Buyers can't push you around. If the top bidder won't honor the top bid, move to the second bid. If that doesn't work out, run another 5-Day sale. In all likelihood you'll sell your home for almost the exact same amount.

Q. Does the 5-Day Method create a "bidding frenzy"?

A. No. Because bidders are in their own homes with only their families, and they have as much time as they need to decide on their bids, bidding frenzies rarely occur. Bids tend to be carefully considered. High bidders are almost always thrilled with their bids. The bids are usually honored.

If the high bidder wishes to rescind the high bid, move immediately to the second bidder.

Q. Should I change the rules for buyers observing sabbath days?

A. No. There are very few individuals who cannot participate in your round-robin on Sunday night for reasons of religious observance. If this does happen, they can designate others to bid for them. Some can not participate Saturday or Sunday, but most can participate one day or the other. That will give them plenty of time to inspect your home and make their decisions.

Q. Why does the 5-Day Method work?

A. The 5-Day Method works because both the buyer and the seller are looking for a fair deal. If there is one thing that characterizes a 5-Day sale (other than the speed of the sale), it's the fact that both the buyer and the seller consider the deal fair. This is why the method works every time. This is why the deals almost always go through.

Q. What if something goes wrong at the last minute?

A. When you run a 5-Day sale you don't have to commit yourself until one day before your sale begins. If you're not ready, or the unexpected happens, you can easily postpone your sale until another weekend that's better for you.

Q. How should I answer brokers who come to the Open House and say my home is going too cheap?

A. This annoying tactic is actually very good for you. Brokers who are trying to disrupt your sale like to make this comment very loudly. When buyers hear it they are encouraged to bid because the broker said the price was too low.

Encourage these brokers to enter the bidding. Tell them you're going to sell your home Sunday night to the highest bidder, and if the home goes cheap they can buy it and make all that extra profit themselves! They never take up this challenge, and that's all you need to know.

If they're not planning to bid, tell them it's time to leave. What they're trying to do is unethical and wrong

SAMPLE MATERIALS

How to Set Them Up

The materials included in this section are samples of the information sheets discussed on pages 81–85, 113–114, 133, 143, and 171. You won't be able to copy them exactly because the information for your own home will be different. Write them as if you were speaking, so when you read them to buyers they won't sound too formal.

Print up 100 copies of each of the sheets. Each topic should be printed on different-colored paper.

Your newspaper ad should be at the top of each sheet. People will show the sheets to other people who have not seen your ad. The other people may come over. They may bid. Don't laugh. I've seen this happen. I've seen the accidental bidder become the buyer.

A home seller recently called me from Houston to tell me about his 5-Day-sale experience. It seems one of the potential buyers couldn't come to the Open House on Saturday because he was hosting a family gathering, so he asked his brother-in-law to make a videotape of the home for him. The brother-in-law ran through the house recording with his camera and brought an awful videotape to the gathering. I'm told it looked like a ship in a storm.

But that didn't stop the entire family from looking at the tape and loving the house. They told the host to be sure to see it on Sunday and bid on it. Unfortunately, the host didn't have enough money and had to drop out of the bidding. So the brother-in-law who shot the tape started bidding, and became the high bidder. His only problem was that he already owned a home and had not planned to move. The seller offered to help him sell his home the following weekend using the 5-Day Method.

Which they did.

Quick Description

LAWRENCEVILLE   BY OWNER

3 Barns—1 Renovated   (7,000 Sq. Ft.)

Pool   Tennis Ct.   Deck   2 Acres

$199,500 or Best Reasonable Offer

Inspection Sat.–Sun. 10–5

House will be sold Sunday Night to

HIGHEST BIDDER   (608) 555-3138

Our home is one of 3 barns built in the 1800s. We renovated the second floor in 1978. To our knowledge, we are the only humans who have lived on this property.

In addition to the large living room, which has a 20-foot-high beamed ceiling, there is a dining room, kitchen, 2 bedrooms, 2½ baths, a workroom, a pool/changing room, a deck overlooking a heated octagonal swimming pool, and a tennis court; all surrounded by perennial gardens and protected by a security system.

The overall size of the house is 2,834 sq. ft., of which we have renovated 1,644 sq. ft. upstairs. Downstairs is 1,190 sq. ft. of finished storage space.

The house has gas heat, central air-conditioning, public water, and public sewer.

The main barn is 2,263 sq. ft. on 2 floors and includes usable stables.

The middle barn is 2,126 sq. ft. on 2 floors and is used for lawn mower storage, etc.

Total square footage of the 3 barns is 7,223 sq. ft.

The estate sits on 2.08 acres.

1993 taxes were $6,162.

To get here, take Rt. 1 to the "Main St.–Princeton" exit (#106). Make a right turn and follow Main St. all the way through Princeton. When Main St. comes to a "T," make a left. We are the 4th house on the right, # 18. Look for the red fence.

Detailed Description

PAWLING   BY OWNER

Country Home

2 Bedrooms   2 Baths   2 Acres

$9,500 or Best Reasonable Offer

Inspection Sat.– Sun. 10–5

House will be sold Sunday Night to

HIGHEST BIDDER   (608) 555-3138

Style:	ranch
Construction:	wood frame
Type of roof:	gable
Roof material:	asphalt
Chimney:	brick
Gutters:	aluminum
Windows:	wood frame, double-pane, double-hung
Storms/Screens:	aluminum
Siding material:	vinyl
Electrical method:	100 amps/110/220 volts/copper wiring/fuses
Heating:	oil/hot water/tank in basement
Water heater:	electric—80 gallon

Water supply:	submersible pump and well	
Waste method:	septic	
Living room:	15 x 15	
Kitchen:	15 x 8	GE 21 ft. Side-by-Side refrigerator
		GE dishwasher
		Magic Chef double wall oven
		Jenn Air grill
Dining room:	13 x 8	
Master bedroom:	17 x 12	double doors/large bathroom
Master bathroom:	8 x 6	
Bedroom 2:	19 x 12	overlooking pond
Bathroom 2:	9 x 6	double sink
Laundry room:	8 x 10	Maytag washer & dryer
Porch:	8 x 8	

Bidding Method

1. Only buyers who have seen the home may bid on it.
2. Bids may be left at any level, at any time prior to 8:00 P.M. Sunday evening.
3. No one can enter the bidding after 8:00 P.M. Sunday evening.
4. The bidding will be open. We will tell anyone the status of the bids at any time.
5. The home will be sold to the highest bidder in round-robin bidding on Sunday night, starting at 8:00 P.M.
6. The highest bidder prior to the round-robin bidding will have the opportunity to make the first bid when the final bidding begins. The next highest bidder will get the second call, and so on down the list.
7. Every bidder will have the opportunity to top the high bid until the highest bidder is established.
8. If there is more than one bid at the same level, the earliest bid will be honored.
9. Bids must be $500 apart ($99,000; $99,500; $100,000; etc.).
10. The highest bidder will be offered the home at the bid price.

Page_____

Telephone Log

(   )   -
_____
_____
_____

(   )   -
_____
_____
_____

(   )   -
_____
_____
_____

(   )   -
_____
_____
_____

Initial Bidding Sheet

Page_____

1. Only people who have inspected our home will be allowed to bid on it.

2. To enter the round-robin bidding you must leave a bid prior to 8:00 P.M. Sunday night.

3. Your initial bid can be any amount. One penny is sufficient.

4. Leave the phone number where you can be reached Sunday night after 8:00 P.M.

5. Initial bids can be telephoned in and changed at any time up to 8:00 P.M. Sunday night.

6. The high bidder on the initial bidding sheet will get the first call in the round-robin. The second highest bidder will get the second call, and so on.

Bidder's Name	Telephone Number	Amount Bid
_____	(___)_____-_____	$_____
_____	(___)_____-_____	$_____
_____	(___)_____-_____	$_____
_____	(___)_____-_____	$_____
_____	(___)_____-_____	$_____
_____	(___)_____-_____	$_____
_____	(___)_____-_____	$_____
_____	(___)_____-_____	$_____
_____	(___)_____-_____	$_____
_____	(___)_____-_____	$_____
_____	(___)_____-_____	$_____

Round-Robin Bidding Sheets

Read to each bidder:

"I will call all interested bidders until there is one high bid, and no other bidder wishes to top it. All bids must be at least $500 apart. If there is more than one bid at the same level, the earlier bid will be honored.

"Currently the high bid is $_____. Do you want to advance the bid?"

Bidder Number	Name	Telephone Number	Bid
1.	_____	_____	$_____
	_____	_____	$_____
	_____	_____	$_____
	_____	_____	$_____
$_____	$_____	$_____	$_____
2.	_____	_____	$_____
	_____	_____	$_____
	_____	_____	$_____
	_____	_____	$_____
$_____	$_____	$_____	$_____

Bidder Number	Name	Telephone Number	Bid
3.	_____	_____	$_____
	_____	_____	$_____
	_____	_____	$_____
	_____	_____	$_____
$_____	$_____	$_____	$_____
4.	_____	_____	$_____
	_____	_____	$_____
	_____	_____	$_____
	_____	_____	$_____
$_____	$_____	$_____	$_____
5.	_____	_____	$_____
	_____	_____	$_____
	_____	_____	$_____
	_____	_____	$_____
$_____	$_____	$_____	$_____
6.	_____	_____	$_____
	_____	_____	$_____
	_____	_____	$_____
	_____	_____	$_____
$_____	$_____	$_____	$_____

Bidder Number	Name	Telephone Number	Bid
7.	_____	_____	$_____
	_____	_____	$_____
	_____	_____	$_____
	_____	_____	$_____
$_____	$_____	$_____	$_____
8.	_____	_____	$_____
	_____	_____	$_____
	_____	_____	$_____
	_____	_____	$_____
$_____	$_____	$_____	$_____
9.	_____	_____	$_____
	_____	_____	$_____
	_____	_____	$_____
	_____	_____	$_____
$_____	$_____	$_____	$_____
10.	_____	_____	$_____
	_____	_____	$_____
	_____	_____	$_____
	_____	_____	$_____
$_____	$_____	$_____	$_____

How to Sell Your Home in 5 Days

Bidder Number	Name	Telephone Number	Bid

11. _____ _____ $_____
_____ _____ $_____
_____ _____ $_____
_____ _____ $_____
$_____ $_____ $_____ $_____

12. _____ _____ $_____
_____ _____ $_____
_____ _____ $_____
_____ _____ $_____
$_____ $_____ $_____ $_____

13. _____ _____ $_____
_____ _____ $_____
_____ _____ $_____
_____ _____ $_____
$_____ $_____ $_____ $_____

14. _____ _____ $_____
_____ _____ $_____
_____ _____ $_____
_____ _____ $_____
$_____ $_____ $_____ $_____

Bidder Number	Name	Telephone Number	Bid
15. _____	_____	$_____
	_____	_____	$_____
	_____	_____	$_____
	_____	_____	$_____
	_____		
$_____	$_____	$_____	$_____

16. _____	_____	$_____
	_____	_____	$_____
	_____	_____	$_____
	_____	_____	$_____
	_____		
$_____	$_____	$_____	$_____

17. _____	_____	$_____
	_____	_____	$_____
	_____	_____	$_____
	_____	_____	$_____
	_____		
$_____	$_____	$_____	$_____

18. _____	_____	$_____
	_____	_____	$_____
	_____	_____	$_____
	_____	_____	$_____
$_____	$_____	$_____	$_____

Open House

CHEVY CHASE   BY OWNER

4BR 3½ Bath New Inside

Rec Rm Liv Rm/Fpl Din Rm Eat-in Kit Den

$399,500 or Best Reasonable Offer

Inspection Sat.–Sun. 10–5

House will be sold Sunday Night to

HIGHEST BIDDER   (608) 555-3138

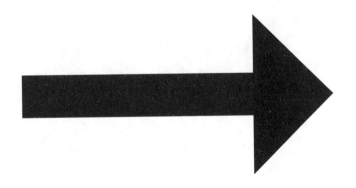

IT SOUNDS SIMPLE BECAUSE IT IS SIMPLE

Checklist

Everything you need to know to run a successful 5-Day sale is in this book. Run down the following checklist. Check off items as you complete them. If you don't understand an item, read about it in the pages indicated.

Item	See Page
____ Are you really ready to sell your home?	45
____ Begin your radon test.	57
____ When do you want to sell your home?	49, 53
____ Will you sell your home furnished or empty?	47
____ How long do you need to move out?	91
____ Have your home inspected.	59
____ Price your home.	67–76
____ Figure out what to fix.	55–65
____ Send radon test to laboratory.	57
____ Fix your home.	63–65
____ Write your ads.	101–103
____ Decide where to place your ads.	97–98
____ Receive radon test results and make copies for buyers.	57
____ Write the rules for your sale.	91
____ Make copies of materials for your sale.	79–80

(Continued on next page)

(Continued from preceding page)

____ Line up friends and relatives if you need them.   115

____ Line up a settlement agent.   207

____ Set up a telephone log.   113

____ Review with your family what everyone's role will be.   115, 135

____ Write a simple set of instructions for how to get to your home.   87

____ Place your ads.   105–106

____ Clean your home.   123

____ Make "Open House" signs.   133–134

____ Know what you'll do if the telephone doesn't start ringing.   181–182

____ Start answering the telephone—read from your script.   117–118

____ Enter every call in your telephone log.   113

____ Get a good night's rest the night before the inspection.   131–132

____ Lay out your materials.   127

____ Set up a bidding list. Be sure to include telephone numbers.   143–144

____ Talk to people when they enter your home. Make sure
everyone gets the printed materials.   135–136

____ Stop the inspection when you say it will stop.   137–138

____ Call your bidders exactly when you told them you'd call.
Read the same information to all bidders.   171–173

____ Get the buyer's settlement agent's name and telephone number.
Give all information about the sale to your settlement agent.   207–208

____ Review the contract with your settlement agent.   209

____ Sign the contract.   210

____ Settle the sale of your home.   211

____ Deposit your check.   212

UNSOLICITED TESTIMONIALS

Thousands of People Have Used This Method!

Since this book was first published, thousands of people have used the 5-Day Method. You can find a 5-Day sale in almost any big-city newspaper on almost any weekend of the year. I've seen a half-dozen 5-Day ads on a single page in *The New York Times.*

People like the method because it works, and because it results in a fair deal for everyone.

When you use the 5-Day Method you pick the exact day you'll sell your home, and exactly when you'll move. You can sell at any time of year. You know when buyers are coming, and you're ready for them. You clean out your home just once. Strangers never go through your home while you're out, and you don't have to leave your keys in a locked box for anyone. The inspection period lasts only two days, and you've picked them to suit your schedule. You sell at a higher price, and you keep the entire proceeds.

You can trust the 5-Day Method. It's more accurate than "comps." It's more accurate than appraisals. It's more accurate than your "real estate professional's best estimate." The 5-Day Method is the best way to know the current value of your home.

It's better for buyers, too. Buyers can stay in your home as long as they like. If they come on Saturday, they can come back again on Sunday with friends and advisers. Buyers really get a chance to go over the home with a fine-tooth comb and no pressure to move on if they like what they see.

They know what they'll have to pay, and they know the house will be sold Sunday night to the highest bidder.

Anyone who's used the 5-Day Method knows it'll work every time. The process is liberating and enjoyable. I've spoken to many individuals who've used it several times. If you use it once you'll never use any other method again.

This method will get you the highest possible price for your home in exactly five days. It results in a fair deal for everyone involved. You'll know you sold your home for the most you could get; and the buyers will know they bought the home for the least they could pay.

Unsoliciticed Testimonials

"Smooth as silk! Thank you. This has given me a whole new opportunity in my life. Everybody was ecstatic. I closed the deal today. . . . This was something else. A sight to behold."

—George Capony, New Orleans, LA

"I saw my sister sell her home in 5 days, and since then I've helped 2 of my friends sell their homes in 5 days. I'm just calling to tell you I think your method is great!"

—Sally Mullikan, Cincinnati, OH

"I'm one of your success stories. I'm calling because you've made a difference in my life and I feel guilty about not personally thanking you for it."

—Mike Williams, Birmingham, AL

"I had extremely good success with your book last weekend, and I'd like to talk to you about using your book in my seminar program teaching real estate brokers how to sell homes."

—Bob Showler, Fairfax, VA

"You were right! It worked! I sold my home in 5 Days!"

—Judith Rawcliff, City Island, NY

"I sold my home using your method 6 months ago. Now I've bought 6 condominiums that I'm selling using the 5-Day Method. If anyone wants to know if this method works, have them call me!"

—Jim Bilavu, San Diego, CA

"Saw you on TV, got your book, did what it said, and sold my home in 5 days."

—Mark Farley, Indianapolis, IN

"The results speak for themselves. I sold my home in 5 Days."

—Ed Jurae, NYC

"I had to sell my mother's Florida home. Someone told me about your book at a dinner party in Jakarta. I priced the home way below what several realtors said they could get for it. I then sold it in five days via your method for exactly what they said it was worth. Thanks to you, I was back in my office the following week!"

—Karen Mills, Jakarta, Indonesia

"I'm very satisfied with the price we got in five days."

—Steve Watson, New Orleans, LA

"This method really works! I sold my parents' home in five days."

—Gary Goldsmith, Lexington, MA

"I wish I had another house to sell. Once the weekend played itself out— exactly as you said it would—I'd love to do it again! It was fun!"

—Richard Spring, Chevy Chase, MD

"Bill, I'm looking at the inside cover of my book, *How to Sell Your Home in 5 Days*. It says 'Jim, give me a call when you sell your home—Bill Effros'"— Well, we sold our home last week, and we're off to California! The book worked just like you said it would."

—Jim Clark, Covington, KY

"I had a business opportunity I couldn't take advantage of unless I sold my home immediately. I saw your book in a bookstore and sold my home the next weekend. Thanks."

—Doug Walker, Salt Lake City, UT

"Just wanted to reach you before the holidays to thank you for helping my dad sell his home. He's so relieved. He's been trying to sell it for 2 years and only 3 people have even come to look at it. The real estate broker said people wouldn't come this far to see a home. Well, we had over 75 people in 2 days! My dad got more than he was hoping for. This is going to add years to his life!"

—David Diamond, Covington, LA

"We sold our home last weekend using your method. Thank God I saw your book in the bookstore!"

—Al Friedman, Chittenden, VT

"We sold our home in 5 Days."

—Carl and Carol Beuhrens,
Oshkosh, WI, on *Donahue*

"Our real estate broker was green with envy. In 5 Days we got 24 bids higher than the highest bid she got for us in 1½ years. You're our hero!"

—Elizabeth and Tim Hunter,
South Burwick, ME

"I just wanted to thank you for your wonderful book. Our house went to contract last evening. It's done, and we now have a firm closing date."

—Dr. Frank Heasley, Ft. Lauderdale, FL

"I'm a builder in Scottsdale, Arizona. We sold the last 2 homes we couldn't sell in our development using your 5 Day Method. From now on we'll sell all our homes your way."

—Brad Huss, Scottsdale, AZ

"We sold my mother's condominium just like you said we would."
—Roberta Kasten, Cranbury, NJ

"My sister just sold her home in Orlando in five days, so I know it works! Now I'm going to sell mine."
—Julianne Sutton, Chicago, IL